WONDERS OF MAN

Published in the United Kingdom by
The Reader's Digest Association Limited, London

THE
TAJ MAHAL

by David Carroll

and the Editors
of the Newsweek Book Division

NEWSWEEK, New York

NEWSWEEK BOOK DIVISION

JOSEPH L. GARDNER   *Editor*

Janet Czarnetzki   *Art Director*

Edwin D. Bayrd, Jr.   *Associate Editor*
Laurie P. Phillips   *Picture Editor*
Eva Galan   *Assistant Editor*
Kathleen Berger   *Copy Editor*
Susan Storer   *Picture Researcher*
Russell Ash   *European Correspondent*

Alvin Garfin   *Publisher*

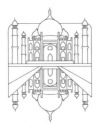

WONDERS OF MAN

MILTON GENDEL   *Consulting Editor*

Mary Ann Joulwan   *Designer, The Taj Mahal*

THE READER'S DIGEST ASSOCIATION LIMITED
25 Berkeley Square London W1X 6AB

London New York Montreal Sydney Cape Town

Endpapers:
*Panels from a seventeenth-century
Mogul court coat; satin embroidered
with a flora and fauna motif.*
  Opposite:
*A nineteenth-century enameled
and jeweled elephant goad made
of chiseled steel.*

Grateful acknowledgment is made to Harcourt Brace Jovanovich, Inc., for permission to quote from *The Travel Diary of a Philosopher* by Hermann Keyserling, translated by J. Holroyd Reece, copyright © 1925 by Harcourt Brace Jovanovich, copyright © 1953 by J. Holroyd Reece.

Contents

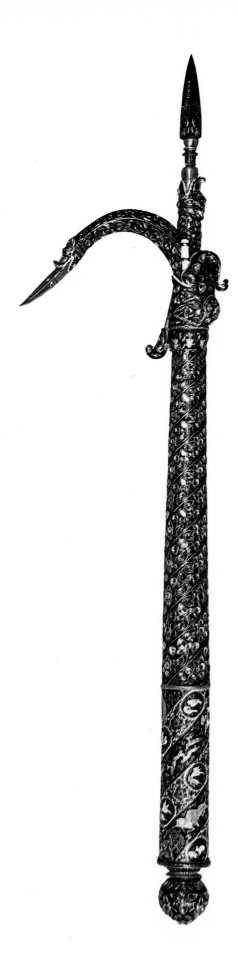

Introduction

Everyone has seen photographs of the Taj Mahal. Indeed, stereotyped frontal views of the renowned Indian monument have become, as the author of the following narrative suggests, one of the great visual clichés of our time. The massive, bulbous central dome, the four slender minarets, the shimmering marble, the long reflecting pool, the manicured gardens — all seem too unreal and, perhaps, too beautiful for adequate description and proper appreciation. But there is much more to the Taj than ineffable loveliness.

The world's best-known mausoleum celebrates one of the greatest love stories of all time — that of the seventeenth-century Mogul emperor, Shah Jahan, and his queen, the "Chosen One of the Palace," Mumtaz Mahal. As a sixteen-year-old prince, according to legend, the future "King of the World" fell in love with Mumtaz at first sight and defied convention by seeking her hand in marriage; he waited five years for their wedding. In their nineteen years of married life, the queen gave Shah Jahan fourteen children. She ruled at his side almost as an equal. Her death in childbirth in 1631, the fourth year of the emperor's reign, left him wild with grief but determined to build history's finest monument to the love of a man for a woman.

Back of this romantic tale is an even more intriguing saga — that of the Mogul conquerors who had swept into North India only a century earlier. By the time of Shah Jahan, they had established an absolute monarchy that is aptly compared to that of his contemporary Louis XIV, the Sun King — half a globe away in France. The Mogul court — located at Agra, Delhi, Lahore, or in the tented encampments used during the dynasty's frequent military campaigns — was incredibly rich, a fact amply attested to by the numerous miniatures that illustrate the text. And it was cruel and sensual as well as omnipotent on the vast subcontinent. As descendants of Tamerlane and Genghis Khan, the Moguls delighted in bloody combat, savage sports, and hideous tortures of their victims. In the absence of primogeniture, brother fought brother for the throne; it was the law of *takht ya takhta* — "throne or coffin." Once crowned, the emperors sought unlimited pleasure in women, wine, and opium. Less than a century after Shah Jahan was deposed by his ruthlessly ambitious son, the dynasty was in irreversible decline. By the beginning of the nineteenth century, all of India was ripe for conquest by Great Britain.

For a time, it seemed as if the Taj — like the Moguls who had built it — would vanish. A scheme to dismantle the tomb and cart its marble back to England for sale was squashed only because of lack of prospective purchasers. The famous grounds became overgrown; the desecrated tomb, a place for picnics and midnight trysts. Only in this century has the Taj been restored to something of its former glory, standing now as a timeless and enduring monument to a vanished empire and to the memory of a great love.

THE EDITORS

Scenes of Indian court life enrich a seventeenth-century cushion cover of painted cotton.

THE TAJ MAHAL
IN HISTORY

I

Chosen One of the Palace

On the hot, flat plains outside Burhanpur the queen lay dead. Her husband's prolonged war against Khan Jahan Lodi was almost at a close and soon the traitor's head would be displayed on a pike high above the city gates. But on this day talk of war was of no interest to the great king — for his queen was dead and he was in despair.

The throne room was empty. Emperor Shah Jahan did not display himself in finely embroidered robes at the royal window that day, nor did he sit with his concubines in the Jasmine Pavilion enjoying the drama of an elephant fight in the riverbeds. He canceled all appointments and went directly to his rooms, where he locked the doors behind him for eight days. During this time he refused to take any food or wine, and the only sound that the ministers who gathered outside his apartments could discern was a low, continuous moan.

On the ninth day the doors opened, and to the surprise of everyone who had known the worldly ruler, Shah Jahan emerged speaking of the impermanence of life and of a desire to renounce his title and become a homeless fakir — this from the same man who, a few years earlier, had cut down four brothers to gain the throne. A strange physical transformation had also taken place: the emperor's back was now bent in a peculiar way and his hair, which had been raven black, had turned totally white. Whispers in the Hall of Public Audience hinted at something even stranger: was it an illusion, or had the emperor grown smaller since the queen's death?

Shah Jahan's unceasing misery wanted company, and he ordered his entire kingdom into mourning. A pall of solemnity hung over North India, and all popular music and public amusements, all perfumes, cosmetics, jewelry, and brightly colored clothes were forbidden. Offenders, no matter what their age or rank, no matter the innocence of their games, were arraigned before a court tribunal; if their behavior was judged disrespectful to the memory of the queen, they were executed. In keeping with his own decrees, Shah Jahan exchanged his royal cape for white robes. His subjects followed his example. Before long the entire country was dressed in white. So intense was this obsessed man's passion for his dead wife that he mourned her for almost two years. It was recorded by an historian that "when she died, he was in danger to die himself."

Half a year after the queen's death, her corpse was brought from Burhanpur to the city of Agra, south of Delhi, which for generations had been the seat of rule for the Mogul Empire (see map, page 31). In Agra, less than a league from the emperor's palace, a silent garden along the banks of a shallow river was chosen as the site for the queen's mausoleum. In the year 1631 the body of Queen Mumtaz Mahal arrived in Agra and was transferred to a temporary crypt in the garden grounds. After prayers were sung for the souls of the dead, work began on the construction of a tomb that would be the most resplendent monument ever built by a man for a woman. But although its brick foundations were laid in 1631, its history — according to one popular legend — can be traced back further, back to Agra on a day in 1607 when a festival was in progress at the Royal Meena Bazaar.

The Royal Meena Bazaar, a private marketplace attached to the palace harem, was in turn a combination royal post exchange and sanctum sanctorum where the women of the aristocracy purchased the dyes, oils, and waxes fundamental to their elaborate toilet. Inside these walls no male dared trespass, for if he were caught he might expect — at the very least — to lose his hands and feet on the executioner's block. However, certain dates were set aside as "contrary days," when everything was done in reverse; and then, for one or two uninhibited days a month, the Royal Meena Bazaar opened wide its gates and became a lusty public pleasure ground.

On such a day everyone was welcome, male and female, royalty and lesser nobility — and anyone of rank or aspiration was certainly there. Most came to indulge in a peculiar game that was customarily played on such occasions. The ordinarily docile wives and concubines of the court reversed their roles and became noisy shopkeepers for the morning, selling trinkets from behind pavilions in the marketplace and flirting and bargaining with the young male courtiers, who — momentarily freed from the suffocating monotony of courtly routine — competed for feminine attentions or showed off their cultured wit by asking prices in rhymed Persian verse. On such days even the emperor himself might arrive, that great Oriental doge who was normally seven times removed from the stream of common life that flowed beneath him. And if he did come, then the Meena Bazaar's rule of the "converse" allowed that even His Majesty was fair target for a discreetly insulting haggle.

At one particular Meena Bazaar in 1607, the vendor hawking silks and glass beads was a newcomer, a girl of fifteen named Arjumand Banu Begam. She was lovely and highborn, the daughter of the prime minister. These facts did not draw customers, however, but instead frightened away the young bloods who ordinarily might have approached the stall of one so fair and well-favored. For the prime minister was Asaf Khan, a powerful and suspicious statesman not to be treated disrespectfully, even on contrary days; only the highest in the land would dare flirt with the daughter of the king's wazir.

On this same day, come to take his pleasure at the Meena Bazaar, was the handsome prince Khurram. Just sixteen, the prince was already a veteran of one war and a poet who could match couplets with the court laureate. His singing voice and his mastery of Koranic calligraphy were both well-regarded, and he had learned the principles of architecture so well that he was often asked to design balconies and municipal warehouses for his father, the emperor Jahangir. If he did at times enjoy attending executions in his father's underground torture chambers, and if he was especially fond of watching the spectacle of death by strangulation, he was, after all, a Mogul prince.

Following the fanfare of his royal arrival, Prince Khurram began to stroll from stall to stall, chatting with his friends and occasionally pausing to inspect the pretty faces, which on any occasion but this would be obscured by veils. Glancing past row upon row of bargaining courtiers and gaily colored tents, he caught a fleeting glimpse of Arjumand positioned near a niche in the corner of the marketplace. Within a moment he was standing at her stall. He wished, he said, to know the price of the large piece of glass on the counter, the one that was cut to look like a diamond. It was indeed a diamond, she facetiously insisted, and its price was high, very high — ten thousand rupees. It was more, she

suggested, than even a prince of such eminence and reputation as he enjoyed could pay.

For a moment Khurram remained motionless, looking steadily at the young woman — wondering, according to legend, why the court gossips who discussed the ladies every afternoon at the underground baths had never spoken the name of Arjumand Banu Begam. Then, without a word, he drew ten thousand rupees from his sleeve, took the piece of glass, turned, and vanished into the crowd, carrying the stone and Arjumand's heart with him.

The following day at the court of Jahangir, the prince applied to the emperor and the emperor's favorite wife for a special favor. He asked for their permission to marry the daughter of the prime minister. It is recorded that when Jahangir heard his son's request he smiled in an oddly mysterious manner and without hesitation raised his right hand in a special gesture which meant that the request was granted.

Arjumand Banu Begam was extraordinarily beautiful — this on the testimony of poets only, for no contemporary likenesses of her are known to exist. Of Khurram we have hundreds of portraits tracing his every posture and change of fortune. Arjumand, however, never sat for a portrait because a Moslem noblewoman did not show her face to commoners, and all painters were commoners. Also, according to *purdah,* the law of the veil, women were obliged to obey Mohammed's command to hide their faces from public glance. The portraits of aristocratic women we do possess are the results of an ingenious circumlocution of this law. The subject sat in one room, facing a mirror from which the painter, who was seated in another room, painted her portrait. Technically he still was not looking directly upon the noble face.

Arjumand was born in her father's harem in 1592 and grew up there in the manner of all daughters of aristocrats. She studied the Moslem holy books, Islam being the official religion of the Moguls (it was a standard part of each child's education to memorize parts of the Koran), and we may assume that she was well-versed in the writings of the Prophet. Further education came from her father and from an even more important political figure, her aunt Nur Mahal, favorite wife of the emperor and the most powerful woman in India. It was to that remarkable woman, who could kill four tigers with five shots and who invented attar of roses perfume, and to the emperor that Khurram had come to ask for Arjumand's hand in marriage. But at the Indian courts marriages of love were unheard of. It was an audacious prince indeed who would inform his father that he had fallen in love and for that reason *alone* wished to marry. Such foolishness was not tolerated. Khurram, however, had a precedent to follow. That tale is part of another history, the legend of Nur Mahal.

It is said that from the moment Jahangir laid eyes on Nur Mahal, he had wanted her. She in turn would not give herself, even to the emperor, except in marriage. There was one impediment to such a marriage — her husband, Sher Afghan, the most powerful general in Jahangir's army. To remove the general from this world the emperor had set a tiger on him, but Sher Afghan reputedly killed it with his bare hands. Stronger tactics were needed and next a wild elephant was let loose on the general, who severed the animal's trunk with one slash of his sword. Forty assassins attacked him;

like Samson, he destroyed them all. But eventually Emperor Jahangir had his way. One night while Sher Afghan slept unguarded in his tent, he was killed by no less than a hundred well-armed henchmen. Then Jahangir wooed and married Nur Mahal. He set her beside him on the throne, a slave to her for the rest of his life while she, using the love-struck emperor as her mouthpiece, became the true ruler of the Mogul Empire. Thus Jahangir could comprehend an all-consuming passion for one woman; thus he smiled in that oddly mysterious manner when his son made his outrageous request.

One year after the request was granted, Prince Khurram was indeed married — but not to Arjumand Banu Begam. His first wife was a Persian princess, Quandari Begam, a relative of the royal family of Persia. If the appearance of this Persian interloper seems to break the romantic sequence, one must bear in mind that in those days members of the royal family could not pick their wedding days and were indeed fortunate if they could pick their wives. The actual wedding dates were at the discretion of the emperor's astrologers, who demanded that all planetary aspects be perfect for state occasions. Likewise, the marriage arrangements of royalty depended on external political considerations, on military coalitions, alliances, fat dowries, or family ties, all of which were first checked against the stars. Then too, Moslem law allowed every man four wives; moreover, any respectable Mogul nobleman, if he did not wish to have his virility or solvency questioned, was expected to keep many concubines as well. For a prince, monogamy was impractical and unacceptable.

For five years Khurram and Arjumand waited. He grew into a startlingly handsome man and she matured into a lady of gentle temperament. For the entire period before their marriage they were not allowed to meet, and they passed the full five years of their engagement without ever once laying eyes on each other again. Finally, on March 27, 1612, when all the calculations of the astrologers were in accord, the long anticipated event took place.

In the center of the marriage procession rode Jahangir and Prince Khurram, surrounded by the *omrahs* and *mansabdars*, officials of the state, some of them wearing for the first and last time robes that had taken six years to embroider. Flanking the royal family were armies of musicians and dancers — and acrobats who rolled alongside the processional as it made its way to the bride's house and back to the palace. From the backs of elephants, ladies in howdahs peeked out at the masses from behind curtains of spun gold, while members of the royal family followed the emperor in silver palanquins, tossing gold mohurs into crowds of onlookers who sometimes trampled one another to death in their rush to reach the coins. All the trappings of the exotic East were present: painted pygmies carrying caged panthers and yellow parrots, long-robed dervishes saying their prayer beads, eunuchs in silks, sweating coolies carrying torches or beating away the crowds that strayed too close to the regal entourage, and muscular black slaves who shooed away flies with elephant-ear fans and chanted songs in an unknown tongue. As the procession swayed gracefully through the balmy night, drummers played the Indian marriage cadence — one deep, monotonous beat repeated over and over again.

The absolute power of the Mogul emperors extended even to matters of romance. When Jahangir, whose likeness is stamped on the gold coin above, fell in love with the wife of Sher Afghan (left), she was soon widowed. The amorous couple below is thought by some scholars to represent Jahangir and his hard-won bride, the beauteous Nur Mahal.

The ceremony, as is customary in Moslem weddings, took place at the home of the bride. At midnight a gigantic feast — attended by the emperor himself, a rare honor — was given. And Jahangir, whose life consisted principally of hunting antelope, drinking large quantities of wine mixed with tincture of opium, torturing men by sewing them into wet animal carcasses, and romancing Nur Mahal — and who, from this bizarre range of worldly experience, had come to consider himself a walking encyclopedia — judged that the charm of Arjumand was incontestable. To show the great esteem he felt for his new daughter-in-law he bestowed on her the highest of honors, a new name. Henceforth she was to be known as Mumtaz Mahal, "Chosen One of the Palace."

After their wedding, the prince was with Mumtaz Mahal day and night. She was beautiful and demure; the royal poets wrote that her loveliness made the moon hide its face in shame, while the stars extinguished their light in fear of being compared to her radiance. She was so intelligent that she soon became a political adviser to her husband. She was charitable, giving food to the peasants and silver to the beggars who called to her each morning outside the brick walls of the palace. She was compassionate, every day drawing up lists of helpless widows and orphans and making certain that the prince attended to their needs. She was generous, supporting hundreds of poor families and arranging pensions for hundreds more. She was, in short, a model of feminine virtue.

Mumtaz Mahal, however, was also of Mogul blood. She enjoyed watching the barbaric torture of prisoners as much as her husband did, and she is said to have

been a cardinal voice behind the brutal religious persecutions of the Portuguese Christians who had settled in Bengal near the site of modern Calcutta.

Of the couple's early life together we know little, but as the years passed Khurram became a successful general with the glory of many victories won for his father in the Deccan — and an eye on the throne. Primogeniture was not always the rule in the Mogul succession; Khurram became the heir presumptive by a process of elimination. His eldest brother, Khusrau, had attempted a rebellion against Jahangir a few years previously. It failed, and Khusrau was placed in irons. Several years later he was turned over to Khurram for execution — after being sent on a ride down an avenue lined with the impaled bodies of his own faithful soldiers. The second brother, Parwiz, died of mysterious causes — some say from drink, some say by the treachery of Khurram. With two brothers out of the way, Khurram had only Jahandar, who was still a child, and his half brother Shahriyar as potential rivals for the throne.

Late in 1627 Jahangir — then fifty-eight years old — was traveling to Lahore from his gardens in Kashmir where he had been taking the mountain air for his chronic asthma. But the ravages of a lifetime spent in debauchery could not so easily be repaired, and along the way Jahangir suffocated from a paroxysm of coughing. Two days after his death, the inevitable struggle for the throne began.

Once, some years earlier, Khurram himself had attempted to seize the throne, but his rebellion had been crushed by the forces of Nur Mahal, who at that time supported Shahriyar's claim to the throne. Now, with Jahangir dead, Nur Mahal again promoted Shahriyar's candidacy. She could easily control the obtuse Shahriyar; he would make an ideal titular figure through which she could continue her rule. But Nur Mahal's hour of ascendancy had passed. After a brief battle in Lahore, Shahriyar's inept generalship lost him the day and within a fortnight Khurram and Mumtaz Mahal marched victoriously into Agra and proclaimed themselves rulers of India.

The coronation took place on February 4, 1628. A pony express system far more efficient than the one used in the American West brought news of the new monarchy to every state in the kingdom — a kingdom that stretched from Assam in the east to Qandahar in the west, from the Upper Deccan in the south to the Pamir Mountains in the north. His kingdom included the largest land area an Indian king had ever ruled. In Agra there were celebrations, gifts, honors. Dignitaries from as far away as Turkey and North Africa attended the ceremony, and trays of diamonds were handed out among the guests. The new emperor awarded a large dowry to Mumtaz Mahal and lesser amounts were shared among his lesser wives. Then, according to tradition, Khurram took a new name to describe the image he held of himself as king: Abul Muzaffar Shihabuddin Mohammed Sahib Qiran-Sani Shah Jahan Badshah Ghazi, henceforth to be abbreviated on less formal occasions to Shah Jahan, "the King of the World."

For those who had supported the new emperor on his way to the throne there were elephants, crystal-hilted daggers, jade drinking cups, Turkish saddles, Ethiopian slaves, and, for some, small kingdoms of their own. For those who had opposed him, there was only the sword. Before his coronation, Shah Jahan had ordered the execution of his two remaining brothers and all his male collateral relatives. Toward Nur Mahal, however, the new emperor was kind, remembering, perhaps, that in his youth she had smiled upon his union with Mumtaz Mahal. Nur Mahal was sent into comfortable exile in the city of Lahore, but for the ex-queen exile was tedium and deprivation of power was death itself. "I am not the moth that dies an instantaneous death," she lamented, "but I suffer a lingering death like the candle that burns through the night without uttering a single moan."

The festivities of the coronation lasted for an entire month. When they were over, Shah Jahan quickly discovered his inheritance to be a vexatious legacy — a considerably overextended empire that already showed troublesome deterioration from the vagaries of his pleasure-loving father's negligent reign. On the other hand, Shah Jahan's private life, his life with Mumtaz Mahal, continued to be idyllic.

The two were inseparable companions by this time, never more than a room removed from each other. He brought her real diamonds now and roses from the finest gardens in India. He took her to the Shalamar Gardens outside Lahore and even brought her along on his military campaigns in the deserts of the south. Eventually he entrusted her with the state seal, the precious Muhr Uzak, a seal so important that once a document was stamped with it even an emperor's commands could not reverse its authority. Shah Jahan built her a magnificent suite of rooms in his palace. Every evening he went there to gain her opinion on a hundred different topics. Soon she was his most trusted

With the wealth of a vast empire at their personal
disposal, the Moguls had ample opportunity to
exercise their taste for opulence. Expert artisans
were commissioned to transform even utilitarian
objects into works of extraordinary beauty. The
mango-shaped crystal box below, threaded with
gold and rubies, was designed to hold pan, an
aromatic mixture of spices and nuts wrapped in
betel leaves. The ubiquitous turbans worn by
noblemen were graced with ornaments such as the
jade piece at right, encrusted with emeralds, rubies,
and white topaz. Perhaps to salve their consciences,
the Moguls instituted the annual practice of
distributing the equivalent of the emperor's weight
in gold and silver to the people. At left, Jahangir
weighs Prince Khurram amid a lavish display of gift
trays spread out on the carpet below them.

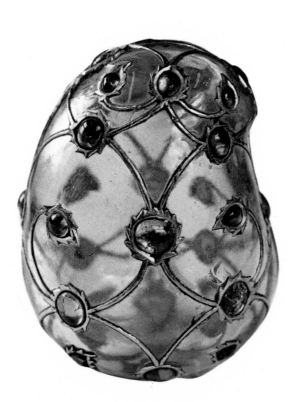

confidante, playing the same political role that Nur Mahal had played with Jahangir, but playing it silently, gracefully, without a trace of her aunt's notorious thirst for power.

During their nineteen years together, Mumtaz Mahal gave Khurram fourteen children, only seven of whom survived. Jahanara, the emperor's favorite daughter and his single companion in the last strange days of his life, was born in 1614. The following year Mohammed Dara Shukoh arrived; he was to be the favorite son. Shah Shuja and another daughter, Roshanara, came next, and Prince Aurangzeb — the hated future emperor of India who would come to power over the bodies of his three brothers — arrived in 1618. In 1624 the future warrior Murad Bakhsh was born. The next three children died in infancy.

In 1630, during the third year of Shah Jahan's reign, Mumtaz Mahal was once again with child. Although she was pregnant, the emperor had allowed her to accompany him on his campaign against Khan Jahan Lodi, a treacherous renegade who had raised a large army in the Deccan.

In the late spring of the next year, in a sprawling cantonment outside the city of Burhanpur, the emperor was directing his troops against Khan Jahan Lodi and simultaneously watching the royal harem for word of his fourteenth child. When the report came, it brought announcement of the birth of a healthy baby girl; but nothing was said of Mumtaz Mahal. For hours Shah Jahan waited impatiently. Still there was no news. A messenger sent to the harem did not return. The alarmed emperor sent another, then a third, but none came back. It grew late, past midnight. Shah Jahan was

preparing to go to the harem himself when at last a message arrived: the queen was well but very tired, and she wished to be permitted to rest undisturbed for the remaining hours of the night.

The emperor was relieved and he too retired for the night, planning to visit the harem in the morning. But a few hours later he was awakened with the unsettling news that Mumtaz Mahal had suffered a relapse and was calling for him. He immediately dressed and made his way through the maze of war tents, arriving at the harem to find a solemn assembly of doctors grouped around the bedside. The queen was dying.

Everyone was immediately dismissed from the room except for Sati-un-nisa, the queen's favorite lady-in-waiting, and Wazir Khan, her beloved doctor. Wazir Khan feared the worst, he told the emperor, for Mumtaz Mahal had earlier confided to him that she had heard her child cry in the womb before its birth, an ominous portent.

For several hours the emperor sat at the bedside and spoke quietly with Mumtaz Mahal. Toward the early hours of the morning she lost consciousness and before the sun rose she was dead.

The story is told — whether it is true or not we will never know — that as Mumtaz Mahal lay dying she whispered in the emperor's ear a final wish. She asked that he build for her a monument of such perfect proportions and of such purity that no one could be in its presence without sensing somewhere within himself the eternal wonder of the power of love and the inevitability of its passing with death. That same year Shah Jahan's workmen began construction of the building complex known as Taj Mahal.

Built as a tomb for his beloved wife, Mumtaz Mahal, the Taj Mahal reveals the most attractive aspect of Shah Jahan's character — his romanticism. The celebrated mausoleum and its four flanking minarets, set on a platform overlooking the Jumna River at Agra, is one of the world's great sights. The view at right was taken from atop the main gateway.

II

New Rulers for India

The city of Agra is located 128 miles south of New Delhi, near enough to the Rajasthani Desert to be buffeted by occasional sandstorms and hot enough, before the cooling monsoon rains, for temperatures to rise above 115 degrees. Agra is poor, like most Indian cities, yet its serpentine thoroughfares bustle with commercial energies. Along those narrow streets, which in truth are lanes carved like deer trails by centuries of passage, one witnesses the daily parade: wooden bullock carts pulled by frothing buffalos, beggars smeared with henna paste, graceful young girls in pastel saris, laughing teenagers speaking English and wearing button-down collars, crippled dogs and scrawny chickens, British taxicabs dented beyond recognition, honking their way through clusters of emaciated cows, long-haired fakirs covered with ash from Siva's fires, ancient, poker-faced merchants sitting cross-legged like shrunken Buddhas, gazing inscrutably at the passing crowds — all are there amidst the sweet smoke of incense and the river's stench. Throngs of Moslems and Hindus push their way through the clamorous bazaar, each living, despite a mélange of haphazard modernization, in the same manner that most Indians have lived for fifty centuries.

Three hundred and fifty years ago this teeming city was the principal capital of the Mogul Empire, but today so completely have all traces of its splendor disappeared that on the banks of the Jumna River, where royalty once erected municipal extravaganzas, one sees only irrigated watermelon patches and dusty ruins.

Not far from the Taj Mahal one such ruin still stands. It is the Rambagh Garden, a place now overgrown with desert creepers and long neglected by a population more concerned with survival than with aesthetics. It is difficult to believe that this scattering of debris was once a verdant garden, and it is even more difficult to comprehend that it was the pleasure ground of a king, the first emperor of the Mogul line. His name was Zahir ud-Din Mohammed, but he was called Baber, "the Tiger."

The Tiger was a mountain man, a bull-shouldered, militant specimen of Turkish ferocity and genius. ("Turkish" in this case refers not to the country of Turkey but to Turkistan, which is located north of Afghanistan and west of the Gobi Desert.) Born high in the steppes of Fergana province, northwest of Afghanistan and 1,500 miles north of India, he at first had no intentions of conquering India, did not like the country when he got there, and went to his grave detesting the Indians. Their languid passivity was puzzling, no doubt, to one of such bellicose ancestry. His father, the king of Fergana, was a descendant of the Turkish conqueror Timur the Lame, or Tamerlane, and his mother was descended from that warrior "born with a clot of blood in his fist," Genghis Khan. When shocked by the indescribable cruelty of Baber and his heirs one need only recall that the blood of these two demonic soldiers ran in Mogul veins, for in fact the word "Mogul" (sometimes spelled Mughal) is derived from the word "Mongol."

Baber's story begins in 1494, when he was eleven years old. One day his father, Umar Shaikh — whom Baber describes as an excellent falconer and one who could make rain with a jade touchstone — was tending pigeons on a platform built over a cliff. The rotted pilings gave way, Umar Shaikh tumbled to his death, and the scepter of Fergana passed to Baber. For the next nine years the young warrior embarked on a career that gave every indication that he was, without doubt, a born loser.

At fourteen, Baber raised an army to storm Samarqand, the legendary city that he would lust after all his life. But no sooner did he possess it than his half brother usurped Fergana, and the Uzbegs of the north drove him from Samarqand. Baber briefly retook Samarqand; but when the Uzbegs counterattacked, he was again routed, his army was destroyed, and he found himself dashing across the steppes to save his life. During this flight he supposedly stopped for the night at the hut of a peasant family, and there a 111-year-old shepherdess recited tales of Hindustan — it was the first time Baber had even heard the name — and told of the innumerable riches waiting there for any man.

With his small band of followers, Baber remained in the hills for many years. His travels took him to Russia and into the Gobi Desert, from whence he contemplated a journey to China. Moving east across Mongolia, he entered a territory ruled by his uncle and left soon afterward with a full-fledged army, lent him by his relative, to recapture the family homeland. He brought his new army southward, into Fergana — and was defeated again. Back to the wilderness went Baber, followed as usual by his retinue of comrades, and there he devised another plan of attack. The city of Kabul in Afghanistan, today that nation's capital, was situated in a valley unprotected on the northern side, where the Hindu Kush Mountains were thought to be an impregnable barrier. In 1504, with the help of Baki, an Afghan king, Baber raised another fighting force, scaled the 12,000-foot passes through the Hindu Kush, marched into Kabul, and in a few bloodless hours proclaimed himself king. He was twenty-one years old.

Baber loved Kabul. He sowed lush flower gardens on its somber brown hills and wandered in the labyrinthine canyons that encircled the city. A model government was established, and many of the sturdy vagabonds who had followed him in his travels were awarded key governmental positions. The arts were thriving in Afghanistan as they never would again, and Baber, a friend of calligraphers and bards, added his verses to theirs and even invented a script, the *Baburikhatt,* which remained in vogue long after his death. If the muses grew tiresome, he knew other, more active forms of entertainment. In the Gardens of Merriment he could referee brawls between the wine drinkers and the opium eaters (he himself was a member of both contingents), watch an elephant gore a rhinoceros, or applaud the skill with which his chief jailer flayed a convicted criminal.

For seven years Baber ruled Kabul. Then, in league with the founder of the Persian Safawid dynasty, which would long rival that of the Moguls in splendor and strength, he attempted to retake Samarqand, failed once again, and returned to Kabul with his dream of northern conquest shattered. He next turned his attention to the land of the Ganges; indeed, it had rarely left his thoughts since that evening when he first heard tales of Hindustan. "From the time I conquered Kabul till now," he wrote in 1526, "I had always been bent on subduing Hindustan." To test the mettle of Indian warriors, he led scouting parties into the Indus valley, and from 1518 to 1525 he engaged the Indians in count-

THE GREAT MOGULS

The first six Mogul emperors of India ruled in an unbroken succession, from father to son, for nearly two hundred years — although the absence of a strong tradition of primogeniture often made the contest for the throne a bloody one. After the death of Aurangzeb, the dynasty went into a rapid decline.

BABER	1526–30
HUMAYUN	1530–56
AKBAR	1556–1605
JAHANGIR	1605–27
SHAH JAHAN	1628–58
AURANGZEB	1658–1707

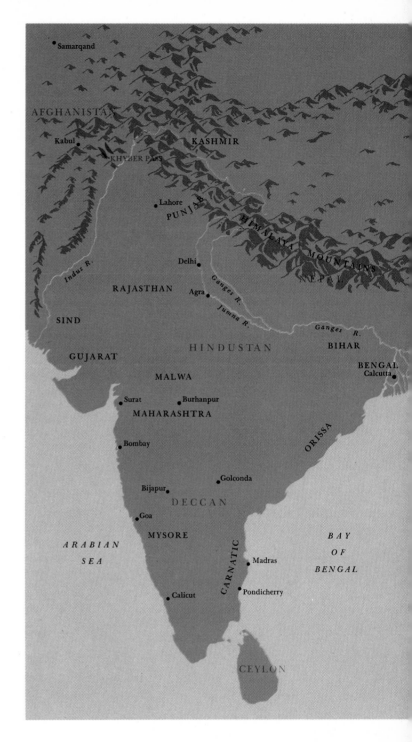

A series of decisive victories, culminating in the battle of Panipat in 1526, made Baber ruler of North India, or Hindustan (see map at right). A miniature from his memoirs (left, below) depicts the northern conqueror's determination in battle. The founder of the Mogul Empire, Baber established a dynasty whose period of glory lasted in an unbroken chain from father to son for nearly two hundred years, as the chart at left indicates.

less skirmishes. They seemed soft enough, or so thought Baber, and he drew up plans for a major invasion.

In 1526, with an army of 12,000 men, Baber marched through the Khyber Pass and onto the North Indian flatlands. North India at that time was ruled by an Afghan king, Sultan Ibrahim, last and least popular ruler of the Lodi family. The unlikable king nevertheless boasted an army 100,000-men strong, and when the opposing forces met on the plains of Panipat near Delhi on April 21, 1526, the northern invaders were outnumbered ten to one. But Baber had a secret, an ancient Chinese invention that the sultan had never seen in his many campaigns — gunpowder. Outflanking Ibrahim's troops, squeezing them between legions of musketeers and mounted bowmen, firing clouds of arrows in Mongol fashion, Baber was able to break the Indian lines at every point. Ibrahim was accidentally slain by one of his own men, and that very evening Baber ascended the throne of Delhi.

Yet Baber was not content with his conquest. The Indian climate was unpredictable, he complained, the food was unpalatable, the inhabitants were listless and uncouth. It was too hot, too dusty, the melons had no flavor, the air was not fit to breathe, nor the water to drink. "Hindustan is a country of few charms," he tells us in his famous memoirs. "Its people have no good looks; of social intercourse, paying and receiving visitors there is none; of genius and capacity none; of manners none; in handicraft and work there is no form or symmetry, method or quality; there are no good horses, no good dogs, no grapes, muskmelons or first rate fruits, no ice or cold water, no good bread or cooked food in the bazaars, no hot baths, no colleges, no candles,

torches or candlesticks . . . there are no running waters in their gardens or residences. These residences have no charm, air, regularity or symmetry . . . peasants and people of low standing go about naked . . . the towns and country of Hindustan are greatly wanting in charm. Its towns are all of one sort; there are no walls to the orchards and most places are in the dead level plain. . . ."

So strong was Baber's prejudice against India and its citizens, whom he considered lackluster, that it was only during the reign of Akbar, his grandson and the first Mogul emperor born on Indian soil, that the after-effects of Baber's anti-Indian sentiment began to vanish.

Suffering equally from the heat and from boredom, Baber traveled to Agra, which his eldest son, Huma-yun, had recently won from the Hindu warrior clans, the Rajputs. There he commenced building a garden that he called the Rambagh, "the Beautiful Garden." A well was dug, zigzag marble channels were arranged to simulate the mountain waterfalls of the Hindu Kush, water was diverted from the Jumna River, flower beds were planted, a bathhouse was constructed — and, according to Baber, "In that charmless and disorderly Hind [India] plots of garden were soon laid out with order and symmetry, with suitable borders and *par-terres* in every corner, and in every border rose and narcissus in perfect arrangement." The Persian garden had come to India. With its symmetrical walkways, running water, central pool, walls and fountains, the Rambagh became a model for other Mogul pleasure grounds and, in time, a blueprint for the gardens of the Taj Mahal.

For Baber, gardens were an evocation of the practical and poetic elements of his character. He reminds one of a Japanese samurai soldier, for whom the gracious arts were as important as the sword. If a battle were to be fought, it must be discovered whether the enemy was a poet; and if so, his verses must be evaluated before the contest began. Baber might halt an entire army on the march to examine an unusual species of plum, and his memoirs, which some consider the finest to come out of India, are filled with the most exacting observations on shells, peacock plumage, storks, wild deer — so much so that the journal reads like a medieval bestiary. His fascination with investigation and his penchant for codifying each detail of nature became a trademark of both Mogul thought and Mogul architecture, which, with its integration of minute detail into enormous geometrical spaces, prompted a critic to remark that the Moguls "built like titans and finished like goldsmiths."

The first of the Moguls, Baber was also the proto-type for the dynasty. In each of his successors can be traced something of the good and something of the evil in his personality. An optimist and idealist, Baber could descend to the realm of the utterly barbaric. A compassionate and tolerant sovereign, he was not above ordering human gladiator fights and jumping into the ring to polish off a loser who died too slowly. Unprovoked murder was not beyond his nature, and like his ancestor Timur, who played polo with the heads of his victims and once ordered his 70,000 soldiers to besiege the Persian city of Isfahan and return bearing one head apiece, he dotted the Indus valley with triumphal mounds of severed heads. Sinister and naïve, surprisingly lenient and unbelievably cruel, a scholar and an

In the sketch at left, a courtier kneels before Baber in his war tent. The haloed figure at right is the emperor's son and successor, Humayun, who was driven from the newly conquered empire in India by the Afghan chieftain Sher Shah.

ignoramus, profoundly religious and highly self-indulgent, Baber expressed all the contradictory characteristics found, each in different measure, in every Mogul emperor who followed him to the throne.

Only four years after coming to India, Baber died in Agra. A strange story is told of his death. His son Humayun became infected with an incurable disease, and hope was abandoned until Baber learned from a Tatar wise man that any desire could be attained provided a man give up his most precious possession for it. Baber considered this possession to be his own life. Promising it to God, he circled Humayun's sickbed three times, at each turn proclaiming his promise. Within days his son had improved and within a few months Baber was dead. The body of the first Mogul was taken to Kabul and there, according to his last desire, it was set in a garden of his own creation. Baber's marble crypt can still be seen today on a hill overlooking the city, not fifty paces from a mosque that his great-great-grandson Shah Jahan built to his memory one hundred years later.

Baber was a stranger to India, one who had come primarily as a despoiler. Consequently his death in 1530 left his successor, Humayun, with an empire of divided loyalties, one that was vast, of dubious borders, and decidedly unfriendly to the Mogul intruders. Indeed, to call it an empire at all is stretching the fact, for the narrow strip of North India, broken into dozens of principalities and ruled over by fiercely independent Afghan warlords, was a complex jumble of warring city-states, akin in its fragmentation to fifteenth-century Italy. In truth, Humayun's only credential for being there at all was his large army, although even that

motley band of Afghan and Persian mercenaries now followed the novice emperor with considerably less loyalty and vigor than they had his free-spirited father.

At the same time the Afghan Lodi princes, members of Sultan Ibrahim's clan — even though they had been solidly thrashed by Baber's hordes — were still strong and ambitious, as were the Hindu Rajput tribes farther south. If Baber had momentarily crippled these warrior clans, he had clearly failed to break their backs. The absence of primogeniture in Moslem society also worked to Humayun's detriment, for his three ambitious brothers, each in quest of the Indian throne, found him an irritating impediment and vied for possession of his head. It was therefore apparent that Baber's victory at Panipat had gained him, at best, a slippery toehold on the Indian subcontinent. And it was equally apparent that to maintain even this tentative suzerainty against a multitude of aggressors who were determined to displace him, Baber's successor must be at least as great a man as he.

Unperturbed by these major challenges and petty vexations, Humayun busied himself with more immediate concerns. In Agra — amidst gilt temples, hanging gardens, temples built to the planets, the largest library in India, and legions of diviners capable of reading the stars above or antelope entrails below — the new emperor sat on a rug as large as a football field, puzzled over conundrums with mathematicians, and wallowed in the fantasies of an opium eater.

Placed by fate on the throne, Humayun never seemed quite certain what to do once he was there, and he ended up following whims, intellectual and hedonistic, which even further removed him from the affairs of

government. Although he was a clever statesman and, when he wished, an excellent soldier, he seemed to prefer the intimacy of palace life. His court became a droll menagerie that contained a spectrum of Oriental curiosities ranging from floating fruit gardens to pigs and horses awarded titles of nobility. Prone to melancholy, compassionate, and passive to the core, he might have preferred the tranquillity of a scholar's cell or the pleasures of a minor pasha's harem to sovereignty over northern India.

In the ranks of Afghan tribesmen there was little sympathy for the new emperor's introversion. A chieftain named Sher Shah arose from the midst of the Afghans and through the power of his charisma organized his people into an enormous fighting force. Quickly assessing the ineptness of the sleeping Mogul, Sher Shah took immediate steps to depose him and return India to Afghan rule. At one time an ally of Baber's, the powerful Afghan had always been a potential threat. "Keep an eye on Sher Shah," Baber once remarked. "He is a clever man, and the marks of royalty are on his forehead." Sher Shah first became master of his own territory, Bihar, next conquered neighboring Bengal, and finally prepared to assault Agra. Humayun knew of Sher Shah's activities but postponed action, foolishly accepting the Afghan's promise not to violate Mogul territory. Soon it was too late. With predictable truculence the Afghans attacked, this time armed with the muskets Sultan Ibrahim's men had been denied fourteen years earlier at Panipat. The Moguls were beaten in two battles, one near Agra, one near Delhi, and in 1540 Humayun was driven from India.

For many years the ex-emperor and a few followers wandered haplessly along the borders of western India seeking aid from local sultans against the Afghans. No funds were forthcoming, however, for although in modern history Sher Shah is named the usurper, to his contemporaries the reinstatement of Afghan power was considered an overdue return of traditional Lodi rulership after the brief and unpopular Mogul interregnum.

During his first years in exile, Humayun traveled to the Punjab in the hope of gaining help from his brother Kamran. But finding Kamran openly hostile to this notion, he retreated southward into the Sind Desert, where in a sort of aimless death march his retinue was reduced to utter desolation. Their horses and camels died in the first months, and their journey to nowhere continued on foot. When the party reached a waterhole or an oasis, men would throw themselves into the wells in a frenzy of thirst, and the animals often drank so much that their stomachs ruptured. At every village they were driven away by local chieftains, who were anxious to curry the favor of Sher Shah.

In 1542, after two years of desert life, Humayun was granted asylum by the raja of Umarkot in the Sind just long enough for his fifteen-year-old wife, Hamida, to give birth to a baby son, Akbar. Soon thereafter the group was forced back into the desert. They wandered throughout the Sind, up into Afghanistan and down again into western India, across what is now Pakistan, and finally into Persia. By the time they arrived in the land of the Safawid courts, nine-tenths of the original party had perished. At that time, the ruler of Persia was Shah Tahmasp, the second Safawid king. Tahmasp, recalling that his father, Shah Ismail, had once been

In the presence of his father and governess, the two-year-old Akbar wrestles with his cousin for possession of a painted drum (left). The adult Akbar played for much higher stakes; on his orders a powerful rival, his foster brother Adham Khan, was thrown to his death from a parapet (below).

allied to Baber — and flattered, we must guess, by having an Indian prince at his doorstep in supplication — welcomed the ragged travelers with extraordinary hospitality. Although not the warrior his father had been — such trust did Shah Ismail's men have in their leader's cause that they sometimes went into battle unarmed — Tahmasp was nevertheless a redoubtable man. He was also an unpredictable one. He once sold a houseguest for 400,000 pieces of gold, he kept his son in a dungeon for two decades, and he was said not to have left the confines of his palace for eleven years. To this bizarre confrontation Humayun brought appropriate humility and, according to legend, the fabulous Koh-i-noor diamond, a stone of 280 carats that was once valued at half the daily expense of the whole world and is today the proudest gem in the British royal collection.

Pleased with this amusing bauble and with Humayun's ingratiating manner, Tahmasp reciprocated in kind, feasted the traveler at a banquet set with 1,500 trays and offered him, between rich amusements, an army with which to conquer India. It was a loan, not a gift, explained Tahmasp, for he wished to return Humayun to India as a servant of the Persian state. For days on end, as he refreshed the Mogul's spirit with condiments and comely slaves, the Shah rehearsed him relentlessly in his forthcoming duties as a Persian vassal. The next year, with a force of 14,000 men, a good cavalry, and portable artillery, Humayun left Persia and headed east. In a drawn-out siege he displaced his brother Kamran from the throne of Kabul and drove him into the Sind in the same manner that Kamran had driven him years before. Next, he turned his attentions

to the more strenuous task of conquering North India.

By this time Sher Shah had been killed in an explosion at an ammunition pile, but during his five-year reign he had established an administrative system of such brilliance that the Moguls would make it the foundation of their government, and even the British would eventually pay it homage. Sher Shah's sons, all men of meager wisdom, were engaged in a dogfight for the throne, and as they squabbled India lay open and unprotected. In 1555, fighting his way through the Khyber Pass and into the Ganges valley, Humayun entered Delhi. In as simple a victory as Sher Shah had won over him fifteen years earlier, he defeated Sher Shah's descendants and reclaimed North India for the Mogul Empire.

Fate, as if to mock Humayun's name — which means "Fortunate" — was consistently unsparing of the second Mogul emperor. On the evening of January 26, 1556, shortly after his triumphant return to Delhi, Humayun was sitting tranquilly on the terrace of his library. The Moslem evening call to prayer was sounded, and as Humayun started down the stairs his foot caught in the folds of his cloak and he toppled headlong down the steps. Within hours, "the melancholy intelligence arrived that the king Humayun had drunk of the last cup from the hands of the Angel of Death."

It seemed that the fortunes of Mogul family affairs had come full circle. As Baber had conquered the Afghans and died before consolidating his position in India, so Humayun had now overthrown the same enemy and passed away with equal speed, leaving his heir, Akbar, as uncertain a legacy as the one bequeathed to Humayun himself twenty-six years earlier.

Akbar was only fourteen the year that his father tumbled to his death, and in accordance with his father's last wishes he was placed under the guardianship of the Persian general Bairam Khan.

Bairam Khan had accompanied Humayun on his desert sojourn, had championed the Mogul cause in Persia, and had led their armies to victory in Delhi. With Humayun gone and Akbar still in his minority, the faithful soldier became the recipient of a strange reward, the interim rulership of an empire. While Bairam Khan signed documents and made war throughout India, apparently relishing his fortuitous acquisition, the genuine heir, Akbar, passed his days in games. With whittled spears and poisoned arrows he stalked tigers in the central Indian jungles. He invented card games, played chess and polo, wrestled, hunted, tamed wild elephants, and outdid his friends at every activity. So absorbed was he in sports that it was said that the best tutors of the palace could not teach Akbar the alphabet, although we know of at least one painting that shows the future emperor perusing a prayer book in wrapt attention.

By the time he turned eighteen, Akbar's tastes in sports had shifted to the game of diplomacy. First he unseated Bairam Khan and sent him on a pilgrimage to Mecca from which the old soldier never returned. Maham Anaga, Akbar's foster mother, was now the only person to whom the young emperor was beholden. But when he discovered that she and her son were plotting his dethronement, Akbar threw the son off a balcony — and when he survived the fall, dragged him up the stairs by the hair and threw him off again. Maham Anaga supposedly died of grief shortly thereafter. Much

to the consternation of a conservative royal council, he then took full command of the empire. Within three years most members of this council were gone and Akbar had begun a program of legislation that has survived, in part, to the present. His kingdom was immature and unshapen, only two generations old. But he had a vision of a united India — and, like his predecessors, he was very ambitious.

Akbar divided his government into thirty-three legislative sections, instituted a land-revenue system, and organized the country into provinces and townships with local officials subordinate to a central government that was located in the Red Fort of Agra, built in 1565. Currency was standardized, new coins were minted, and all political appointments were arranged by imperial decree. Land was reclassified and graded for fertility, and a reasonable tariff system was levied, doing away with taxation on those who could not pay and increasing it on those who could. Peasants were reimbursed for damages done to their lands by military incursions, and taxes on basic foodstuffs were abolished. Akbar invented a new system of weights and measures and instituted a mail system and a pony express. He outlawed child marriages and infanticide, made the keeping of local administrative records obligatory, recruited an army, set up a civil service, planted shade trees that still stand today, built roads, temples, forts, inns, way stations for travelers, whole cities — in short, he created an empire.

The most farsighted of his reforms was the exemption of Hindus from the taxes and indignities that had harassed them for centuries in Moslem-controlled North India. Then as now, India was a Hindu nation,

and the Moslem invaders who had come in 712 gained control over, but never the allegiance of, the Hindu majority. Akbar realized that the Hindus were a potential ally. In 1564, he outlawed the desecration of Hindu temples, rescinded the *jizya*, a poll tax on non-Moslems, and banned such immensely degrading policies as the right of a Moslem magistrate to spit in the mouth of a Hindu who was late in paying his taxes. Rajput kings were elevated to high public office. Although Akbar did not hesitate to make war on those Hindus who defied him, he also raised the sultans he conquered to governorships and sometimes, to cement such partnerships, he even married their daughters.

To enlarge and maintain his new empire, Akbar found it was necessary to wage war, or so he told his biographer, Abu-l Fazl. With Machiavellian amorality he declared, "A monarch should be ever intent on conquest, otherwise his enemies would rise in arms against him." This logic was hard to dispute amidst the warlike Hindus, and consequently the Moguls were incessantly on the offensive. The Punjab, Gwalior, Jaunpur, Malwa, Chittoor, Gujarat, Bengal, Kabul, Kashmir, the Sind, Qandahar, part of Ahmadnagar, Gondwana, Berar, Asirgarh, and a dozen lesser territories fell to the Moguls in the period between 1557 and 1601.

Dressed in golden armor and mounted on an elephant or charger, Akbar habitually stationed himself in the center of the most ferocious fighting. His generalship was unorthodox and brilliant: he was a master of the surprise attack, the forced march, the hit-and-run. When not in the field, he kept fresh blood on his

soldiers' swords by taking them on long jungle hunts,
during which as many as ten thousand animals would
be flushed from the bush and hacked to bits. Akbar's
numerous inventions include three varieties of the
matchlock rifle, a portable war tent with two bedrooms,
a primitive machine gun that fired fourteen rifles
simultaneously, a system of river transportation in
which elephants and large weapons were floated on
pontoons to their destination, and a cannon so large a
thousand oxen were needed to transport it. So mighty
was this third Mogul emperor, so seemingly invulnerable was he in a day when men saw no paradox in the
concept of the warrior-saint, that soldiers on both sides
began to think him invincible. Akbar did not deny it.
It was divine protection, he said, due not to his own
merits — he was, after all, a humble man — but to an
invisible shield that God had girded him with at birth.

Akbar was in fact an extremely religious man. Born
a Moslem, he soon grew disillusioned with the dogma
of orthodox Islam and began investigating the alternatives. At eighteen, disgusted with the materialistic life
at court, he set out alone into the desert. There he
claimed to have been visited by a divine voice. From
that moment, Akbar began a search for spiritual truths,
a search that was to become an obsession with him. To
enshrine his religious quest he built the Ibadat Khana,
"the House of Worship," to which he invited theolo-
gians from all over the world. Soon its courtyards were
filled with exotic divines from different lands and
representing almost every major religion then known
to man. The emperor kept these men constantly in his
company; he listened intently to each of them, but he
remained uncommitted.

One day, to the puzzlement of almost everyone, Akbar seemed to have embraced all the religions of the world simultaneously. He appeared in council with the Hindu tilak mark on his forehead and celebrated the festival of Dewali with the ardency of a devout Brahmin. The next day, he wore the girdle of the Parsis (the Indian practitioners of Zoroastrianism) and prostrated himself before the sun in the typical Parsi manner, expecting all others to follow his example. Jain devotees convinced him of the validity of nonviolence, and the emperor passed laws restricting the slaughter of animals for food. Prophets of the Sikh religion were given an audience; they found the emperor "an attentive listener." Taoist and Confucian scholars arrived from China, Sufis from Bukhara, Hinayana monks from Ceylon. In the center of the courtyard, the emperor had a raised sandstone platform built for the preparation of astrological readings. He consulted magicians, learned physiognomy from Hindu fakirs and alchemy from Arabs. On certain nights the two Brahmins, Debi and Purushottama, were hoisted up on a scaffold outside Akbar's bedroom where, with the two wise men suspended over the harem courtyard and the emperor seated on the window ledge, metaphysical conversations continued until dawn.

Akbar had long been fascinated with Western religions, and in 1578 he sent to the Portuguese colony of Goa for representatives of Catholicism. Soon the Italian Rudolfo Aquaviva and the Spaniard Antonio Monserrate arrived at court. They were young men, enthusiastic for disciples and anxious to convert the heathen ruler to their faith or die in blessed martyrdom in the attempt. To their amazement, the great barbarian was as urbane as any Umbrian nobleman. He greeted them with overwhelming reverence, and this caught both clerics by surprise. Then, publicly kissing a copy of the Plantin Bible, he led them into his private chambers, where he hung an enormous crucifix over his bed and a miniature cross around his neck. The priests were given a suite of handsome rooms, and Akbar came to them regularly for religious instruction. He was seen every afternoon in the gardens with his heavy arm on Aquaviva's shoulders, questioning him on doctrinal interpretations or attempting to recite the day's catechism in Italian. At first the priests were baffled. Soon their shock turned to exhilaration. This pagan, the lord of millions of unsaved souls, stood on the verge of baptism. Here was Clovis, here was Constantine himself! Had not the emperor announced that he was on the very eve of his conversion, and had he not promised that all his heathen hordes would follow? Such a conversion would be worthy of sainthood.

Time passed. The emperor was ever ardent in his worship of the cross and in his demonstrations of affection for the priests. Yet he managed to evade the question of conversion. A year went by, then another, while Akbar assiduously studied the Scriptures. The priests waited. Life became uncomfortable for them at the palace. The Mogul courtiers were not friends of Christianity, nor were the townsmen at large. Akbar disappeared for months at a time on military excursions, leaving the clerics to fend for themselves against antagonistic rivals. Impatient inquiries came from Goa: why had they not gotten on with the conversion? The puzzled priests continued to receive a river of imperial favors, they continued to press for a favorable response, and they continued to wait for some royal sign.

The Oriental way of saying yes or no is rarely executed with a direct reply. It was not till many years later that the missionaries understood that Akbar's very act of postponement was an indication of refusal. Surely the Moslems would not have tolerated the conversion of their emperor to Christianity, nor was Akbar willing to jeopardize his Hindu alliances by embracing a creed opposed to the fundamental precepts of his allies. And certainly there was no material gain to be earned from such a change. The few Westerners who had come to Agra came in unimpressive style bearing mundane gifts and empty promises. Realizing the fruitlessness of their labors, Aquaviva and Monserrate sadly returned to Goa. There Aquaviva, apparently still intent on martyrdom, was murdered by an angry mob of Hindus while preaching the Gospel.

Perhaps Akbar felt that Christianity contained a certain quality of Gothic fervor missing from the more intellectual Oriental religions with which he was familiar. Or perhaps the two priests were but another curiosity to an emperor who was always anxious for diversion. Whatever the case may be, toward the middle of his life, after refining his version of the spiritual doctrines he found credible, Akbar announced the formation of his *own* religion, the Din-i-Ilahi, and he invited all of India to join. The tenets of the Din-i-Ilahi were simple: prayer was said three times a day; all meat was avoided at table; the principles of reincarnation and karma were accepted; a soft voice and gentle words were recommended for conducting daily communications; and forgiveness, toleration, and kindness toward all living creatures were stressed. Ten virtues were to

be followed, ten vices shunned. The sun was worshiped as the body of the Divine, and unification with God was the ultimate goal. There was no priesthood, no clergy. Akbar alone was the Holy Magnifying Glass through which the rays of the sun were focused onto humanity. He was, in essence, a god on earth. *"Allahu Akbar"* was stamped on his coins; and since "Akbar" also means "great," the phrase could be read either as "God is great" or "Akbar is God."

At first it seemed that the monarch would succeed in one of the most difficult of all human endeavors, founding a religion that lasts beyond the death of its creator. Lords and peasants alike agreed to conversion. But adoption of the Din-i-Ilahi meant forsaking ancient beliefs, plus a tacit acceptance of Akbar as a god, and many were hesitant to go that far. Traditionally, Hindus considered kings divinely inspired, representatives of higher powers, but not gods per se. To forsake their cosmic deities for the worship of a mere mortal was too much to ask. And the Moslems, forbidden in the Koran to pay homage even to the image of a man, balked wholeheartedly at the veneration of a living one. The Din-i-Ilahi dragged on for some time with a few of the faithful remaining in attendance, but when Akbar died his church died with him.

In an oblique way it was Akbar's dedication to religion that determined the construction of the greatest Mogul city ever built. As the emperor grew older, his concern over the absence of a male heir became his principal anxiety. Learning of a dervish named Shaikh Salim Chishti, last of the many great sages in the Chishti line, Akbar journeyed to see him in the tiny town of Sikri, twenty-three miles west of Agra. Shaikh Salim

In Shaikh Salim's honor, Akbar constructed an entire city on the site of the wise man's hillside hermitage. The governing center of Fatehpur Sikri was the audience hall. From a circular platform atop a richly decorated pillar (left) Akbar received reports from noblemen seated on four adjoining balconies. At right is the courtyard of the mosque at Fatehpur Sikri, as deserted today as it was in 1585 when the impetuous emperor irrevocably abandoned his artificial creation after only fifteen years' residence there.

recited blessings and made promises, and in 1569, soon after their meeting, Akbar's Hindu wife gave birth to a son, Salim, later to be known as Jahangir. Then came two additional sons, Murad and Daniyal.

Akbar's response to Shaikh Salim's magic must rank as one of the outstanding examples in history of royal gratitude. He commanded a city to be built on the spot where the saint's retreat was situated, and Shaikh Salim was made spiritual mentor of the entire metropolis.

Almost overnight an army of laborers was mobilized to fashion the city of Akbar's dreams. "His majesty plans splendid edifices," wrote Abu-l Fazl, "and dresses the work of his mind and heart in the garment of stone and clay." By 1570 the construction, using a sort of prefabrication technique, was in full swing. "The house when it was in building," wrote Father Monserrate, "was built of stone made ready before it was brought thither: so that there was neither hammer nor axe nor any tool nor iron heard in the house while it was in building." Most of the city was completed in seven years, a remarkably short time when we consider that the Taj Mahal alone took twenty-two years to construct.

Akbar designed many of the structures himself and worked in the pits with the stonemasons, cutting bricks and carving sandstone corbels. Huge battlements and a wall with nine gates appeared. The five-story mosque known as the Panch Mahal was later constructed in the style of a Buddhist temple. A huge rectangular courtyard was erected, bounded by symmetrical gardens. Three palaces, waterworks and baths, a mint for stamping coins with Akbar's profile, a Turkish palace for Akbar's Turkish wife, a Hindu palace for Akbar's Hindu wives, a Moslem palace for Akbar's Moslem wives, an enameled hall for the emperor to play hide-and-seek with all his wives, a court on which to play pachisi with human pieces, private residences, viaducts, stables, octagonal towers, domed pigeon houses — all appeared as the most perfect examples of their kind in Mogul India. There were other things of interest, too: the first Indian hospital, a seventy-foot octagonal tower built in honor of a pet elephant, an artificial lake, a girls' school, a zoo, a sewage system, and the largest gateway in the East, the Buland Darwaza, which served as entrance to a city described by a Western traveler, Ralph Fitch, as "greater than London and very populous." It was named Fatehpur Sikri, adding the word for victory to the original name of Shaikh Salim's village.

In Fatehpur Sikri, Akbar gathered the finest singers, the boldest statesmen, the wisest philosophers, artists of such skill that they were considered holy. His cabinet, known as "the Nine Gems," was reputed to hold the nine most capable men in the world. One was a brilliant financier, another a military genius allegedly able to appear simultaneously in two locations on the battlefield. Another was the poet Faizi, whose brother Abu-l Fazl wrote *Akbar Namah,* the most poetically penned biography of the period. Another was Tansen, a singer who was fabled to have understood the principles of vibration so thoroughly that when he sang "Song of the Lamp" his voice kindled wood. Every day these men gathered in the throne room, and there, surrounded by ministers, sons, wives, advisers, soldiers, ambassadors, and thousands of subjects who struggled to catch sight of his face, on a throne carved in the shape of a lotus, Akbar held court.

A day in the life of the emperor found him engaged in a hundred pursuits. His energy was illimitable — he slept only three hours a night — and it was said that there was nothing that he did not know how to do. He was obsessively curious. He imported rare plants and grasses, grafted trees, crossbred doves, and maintained zoological notebooks as Baber had. He sent for a Western pipe organ and taught himself to play it, and he commissioned translations of Aristotle and the Greek philosophers. To test the Moslem claim that Arabic was the language all men would speak from birth if not taught otherwise, he isolated twenty newborn infants in a cave and raised them for five years in the care of silent nurses. (Five years later, as expected, twenty dumb innocents emerged.) Akbar wrote letters to a number of famous people including the pope and two Spanish kings, and the first Anglo-Indian diplomatic relationship was established when the emperor corresponded with Queen Elizabeth I.

At Fatehpur Sikri, Akbar set up *karkhanas*, or trade guilds, in which thousands of craftsmen were trained in over seventy occupations. His favorite branch of this institution was the painters' studio, and it was at Fatehpur Sikri that an art specifically Mogul really began to develop. The painters in his ateliers were well-paid and well-pampered. They were soon joined by a multitude of artists from all over Asia, lured to the monarch's court by tales of wealth and a great king's patronage. The rank of painter had traditionally been a low one in Moslem India, where to create the likeness of a man was considered a preemption of the Creator's prerogative. But with some nimble theological reasoning, Akbar deemed painting a sacred discipline on the grounds that it demonstrated how poor were man's attempts to imitate the works of God. To prove his point, he kept thousands of painters busy night and day manufacturing such imperfections, honored the most talented of them with high-sounding names like "Sweet Pen," and "Wonder of the Age," and even posed for their compositions — and by so doing introduced portraiture to Indian art. No wonder that architects, masons, calligraphers, and laborers of all races migrated to his court, and that many remained, some raising children who in time would help build the Taj Mahal.

After fifteen years of life at Fatehpur Sikri, the fickle sovereign began to grow bored with his magnificent project. The harsh landscape around Sikri was not conducive to gaiety, and drinking water was inaccessible (a man-made lake, dug nearby, collected only brackish water). In 1585, when a military campaign called him to Northwest India, he moved his headquarters to Lahore and left Fatehpur Sikri forever. The story that Akbar deserted this city to oblige Shaikh Salim when he complained that the noise was disturbing his devotions is apocryphal, for Salim had died some years before Fatehpur Sikri was abandoned.

As quickly as it had been populated, the magnificent city was emptied. A few years later, it was described by a European as "ruinate, lying like a waste district, and very dangerous to pass through at night." Today, except for a small community at the foot of the city that lives off the largess of occasional tourists, Fatehpur Sikri is unoccupied, a ghostly red and white necropolis of sandstone courtyards and endless silent corridors, all in a state of perfect preservation. Its preservation, indeed, seems almost too perfect, and the

स्वामिहरिदासजी

ingredients of the time-resilient mortar used between the bricks have never been chemically analyzed with any real success.

As Akbar grew older, legends formed around his name. People claimed that his breath could heal, and they brought their children to court to be breathed upon by the emperor. Like the Buddha, he was supposed to have delivered a speech from the cradle. He could command the clouds to disperse or give rain, they said, and it was rumored, as it has been with so many Eastern kings, that at night he secretly wandered the streets of the city noting injustices and punishing offenders when he returned to the palace. The last years of this powerful and revered emperor were nonetheless troubled and unfulfilled. His sons Murad and Daniyal became heir to a common Mogul disease — alcoholism — and both died of delirium tremens. Young Salim also grew into a dissipate. Furthermore, there was no question that the Din-i-Ilahi had failed, that alliances were being broken across India, and that conquered territories were everywhere on the verge of rebellion. Worse yet, many of Akbar's closest friends died in close succession. By his own admission, he had failed to attain the spiritual goals he had set for himself as a young man. Tired and disillusioned, the great monarch died of dysentery in 1605 and was buried six miles northwest of Agra.

Akbar's tomb at Sikandra is set in a large garden. It is as Hindu as it is Moslem, as Buddhist as it is Persian, an eclectic image of the eclectic man who lies beneath its dark, empty chambers. As ruler of India for forty-nine years, he came as close as any man in history to uniting the subcontinent. And no doubt he also fulfilled the expectations of his father, Humayun, who in the years of his desert exile, unable to award his followers the gifts customarily due at the birth of a prince, handed them musk saying, "This is all the present I can afford to make you on this birth of my son whose fame will, I trust, be one day expanded all over the world as the perfume of the musk now fills this tent."

At the time of the greatly renowned sovereign's death, Salim, who had already developed a reputation for unsavory behavior by staging a pointless rebellion against his father, was the only one of Akbar's sons eligible for the crown. Upon coming to the throne in 1605, the thirty-six-year-old prince took the name Jahangir, "the World Seizer," modestly recording in his memoirs that "I thought it incumbent on me to assume at my accession that [name] of Jahangir Padshah [The King Who Seizes the World] as the title which best suited my character." He was short and squat with slanted eyes, husky Mogul shoulders, and a thin mustache which he combed downward to prevent it from pointing at heaven, a divine insubordination in Islam. His inheritance was a territory that took "two years travell with caravan" to cross.

In the beginning, Jahangir's ambitions were admirable. He installed a huge bell attached to a gold chain in the Hall of Justice and announced that anyone seeking justice was to ring it for an immediate royal audience. He instituted twelve edicts that guaranteed his people rights to government hospitals, freedom from certain unfair tax foreclosures, the reversion of a deceased's property to his heirs, and the abolition of harsh punishments, such as the slicing off of the nose for any number of petty crimes. All of Jahangir's re-

Jahangir's interest in portraiture was fostered in his father's studios at Fatehpur Sikri. In his zeal for accuracy he even sent a painter to Persia for a likeness of Shah Abbas that was later incorporated into an allegorical painting (left, below). Although the two rulers embrace in symbolic fraternity atop a globe of the world, Jahangir's larger size and the fact that his symbol, the lion, threatens to drive the Persian lamb into the Mediterranean reveal his true aims. Mogul ruthlessness is attested to in a drawing (right) of one of many towers studded with the severed heads of India's enemies.

forms were considered liberal measures for their day.

Gradually, however, things went wrong. Jahangir persecuted the Jains and brought the new but already influential sect of the Sikhs to the verge of rebellion by executing their leader — in this way reviving the religious intolerance his father had so earnestly tried to overcome. A fickle and angry temperament alienated his potential supporters; an alternately ruthless and sentimental one drove them from his doors. Neglecting his duties, he withdrew to the company of idle fops and sycophants; growing bored with them, he found stimulation in the execution of criminals. He had prisoners flayed alive or had them sewn into wet buffalo skins, which slowly shrank and suffocated the man within; he ordered men thrown beneath elephants, but wept for the elephants because they shivered in the cold. Perpetually drunk, he boasted of his enormous capacity. Then, in schizophrenic transformation, he outlawed wine, wrote treatises on its harmful effects, penalized all offenders with hideous punishments, and vowed to every witness, terrestial and divine, that he was done with intoxicants forever. Within a month he returned to twenty-one cups a day.

During the first five years of Jahangir's reign, his palace became populated with all manner of freaks, clowns, and other bizarre hangers-on. There every strange new entertainment was welcome. The court lived in a self-contained dreamworld where the word "death" was outlawed. Courtiers followed the emperor everywhere, bursting into ecstatic applause when he gave an order or recited an impromptu poem. "The collar, my love, has not been dyed with saffron: engraved therein is the pallor of my face," Jahangir would improvise,

and immediately a dozen obsequious nobles would attempt to outdo one another in the eloquence of their praise. The emperor in turn handed out gifts and bestowed awards of rank and applause. But to attend the emperor was to sleep with a tiger. Men were executed for the pettiest of crimes, lords rose and fell according to Jahangir's daily turn of mind, and if he were not in a good humor, woe to all men of ambition and those inclined to scheme.

To the courts of this strange man came two adventurers, their arrival coinciding with the beginnings of British influence in India. The first was the "bluff seadog" William Hawkins, captain of the frigate *Hector*, one of the first English crafts to cruise the west coast of India; the other was Sir Thomas Roe, the reserved ambassador of King James I to the Mogul court. Possessed of polar temperaments, these men provide two points of view on the same society. From Roe, we hear of the politics that took place at the Mogul court; from Hawkins, of life in the emperor's sitting rooms and in his boudoir.

William Hawkins was a professional soldier of fortune, a womanizer and an opportunist, a smooth talker and a devout alcoholic. Appearing for the first time before Jahangir with no greater gift than a bolt of common broadcloth, he immediately caught the monarch's fancy. Jahangir plied him with a hundred questions and before the interview was over, Hawkins had been invited to remain at the court as "resident ambassador." Presently he was wearing the clothes of a Moslem aristocrat and was being addressed as Khan Hawkins. Jahangir gave him an Armenian concubine and access to the royal table where, as the emperor's

number one drinking companion, Hawkins told bawdy stories that made Jahangir shriek with laughter. For a year the sailor and the emperor were inseparable.

While Hawkins played the stooge for Jahangir, he was at the same time recording his impressions of the emperor, whom he saw with few illusions. "The King is thought to be the greatest emperor of the East for wealth, land and force of men," he wrote, adding that Jahangir was "ill-beloved of the greater part of his subjects who stand greatly in feare of him." Hawkins watched as the monarch executed his own secretary on the mere suspicion of disloyalty. A soldier who asked too high a salary was forced to wrestle a caged lioness and was followed to extinction by ten unlucky by-standers, ordered willy-nilly into the cage by a drunken Jahangir. Another man was beaten by twenty guards for breaking a porcelain cup — and was then sent to China to replace it. In a rage over a minor disobedience, Jahangir stabbed his son Shahriyar in the neck with a bodkin. He appeared in court surrounded by an entourage of hooded henchmen bearing axes and whips, "readie to do the King's bidding." In his harem were five thousand women, maintained on a budget of thirty thousand rupees a day; and in the interior rooms, separated from the three hundred royal wives by thick partitions, one thousand young men awaited Jahangir's alternate pleasures. Outside the harem, in a different kind of stable, were the emperor's animals, a veritable zoological garden. There were twelve thousand elephants, ten thousand oxen, two thousand camels, three thousand deer, four thousand dogs, one hundred tame lions, five hundred buffalo, and ten thousand carrier pigeons.

For two years Hawkins was in the emperor's favor, but after that time his influence slowly declined. Jealousy on the part of other noblemen weakened his position, as did Jahangir's inconstant attentions, which were based as much on who amused him as upon who served him. When the wily mariner saw the last remnants of his prestige slip away, he too slipped away — only to have death overtake him before he could reach his native England.

In sharp contrast to Hawkins, Thomas Roe was refined and effete, a British gentleman and an aloof chronicler of human nature. Never joining the charmed circle of the emperor's inner court, he remained outside, peering in with penetrating eyes and marking down his observations in letters written to his superiors in England. Noting Jahangir's weakness for fine arts, he won him over at the bargaining table by promising him English treasures, "payntings, carvings, cutting, enamelling, figures in brasse, copper and stone, rich embroideryes, stuffs of gold, and silver," all in return for a single request — the establishment of trade between England and India. Jahangir could foresee no danger in dealing with the British, whom he judged simpleminded, and he accepted.

Continuing to play on the Mogul's weakness for paintings, Roe showed the emperor a collection of miniatures, which Jahangir found astounding. Jahangir then astounded Roe by having his painters copy the pictures so expertly that Roe was unable to choose between the copies and the originals. Before long, however, Jahangir became fascinated with European art, and his infatuation can still be seen in the Mogul paintings of the time. They are filled with Venetian

49

wine glasses, caryatids, men dressed in British costume, *putti* bearing hourglasses, and renderings of the Virgin Mary. Satisfied with success on many levels — though he had failed in his primary objective of negotiating a formal treaty with Jahangir — Thomas Roe returned to Britain in 1618.

In view of Akbar's fascination with Christianity, it is not surprising that images of the Virgin should appear at the court of his son; and it was even said that of all Mogul rulers, Jahangir came closest to embracing Catholicism. Although publicly a Moslem, Jahangir wore a locket with a picture of Jesus, attended mass at the Catholic church built by Akbar in Agra, and called on his deathbed for the rites of Extreme Unction.

From the stories that are told of him, both Moslem and Christian, we must assume that religion for Jahangir was but another form of entertainment. For example, when the Moslem elders warned Jahangir that the Koran forbade the eating of certain meats, the emperor was offended and told them that he was converting to Christianity, which had no such bothersome rules. He sent for European tailors, had Elizabethan cap and breeches cut, and prepared to take the sacraments. The elders finally relented and allowed that His Majesty was, after all, above Koranic law and might partake of all the meat he wished. In another incident, Jahangir, puzzling over the relative merits of the Mohammedan and Christian religions, came up with a brilliant manner of judging between them. He ordered a Moslem and a Florentine priest to jump into a roaring bonfire and promised that he would embrace the creed of the man who was not consumed. And in yet another incident, Jahangir decided to establish the true

By 1620 Jahangir's gifted queen, Nur Mahal, was the virtual ruler of Mogul India. When her father — who served as chief minister and was known as Itimad-ud-Dowlah, or "Pillar of the State" — died two years later, she had an elaborate white marble tomb constructed for him at Agra (below).

religion by taking the names of twelve faiths, putting them in a hat, and procuring a blindfolded gorilla to pick a name. According to the story, the simian arbitrator did just that, three times choosing the name of Christianity and the fourth time refusing to pick at all when the name of Christianity was surreptitiously removed from the hat.

Passing his days in such amusements, the fourth Mogul emperor slowly grew indifferent to public matters of any sort. By the time his liaison with Nur Mahal began, he was happily prepared to relinquish all immediate political responsibilities to one who found them more amusing. "All I desire," he said in the spirit of Omar Khayyám, "is a cup of wine and a piece of meat. To rule the kingdom I have Nur Mahal." Nur Mahal was indeed an astonishing lady, one who was capable, in a country where women were locked behind veils and harem walls, of superseding all convention. A Persian, she was born Mihr-un-Nisa and traveled as a child to India with her father, Ghiyas Beg. Along the way they were befriended by the caravan master Malik Masud, who introduced them to Akbar. Within a few years, the able Ghiyas Beg had worked his way up to the position of *diwan*, or treasurer, of Kabul. When Akbar died, Ghiyas Beg stayed on to serve Jahangir; and when Nur Mahal became queen, Ghiyas was promoted to the highest post in the land and given the title Itimad-ud-Dowlah, "Pillar of the State." His white marble tomb in Agra, with its expertly carved lattice windows and inlays of precious stones, is a magnificent rectangular jewel box. It still bears his honorary title, the tomb of Itimad-ud-Dowlah, and from its minarets one can easily see the Taj Mahal itself.

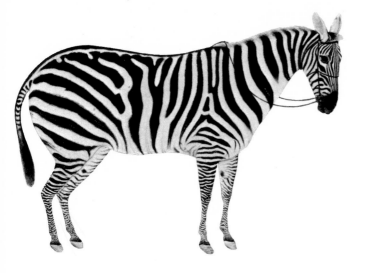

Jahangir Padshah means "the king who seizes the world" — and as the World Seizer himself observed, the name he assumed when he succeeded to the Mogul throne was well-suited to his character. The formal portrait below shows Jahangir hefting a small but highly symbolic globe. Like Baber and Akbar before him, Jahangir was an ardent amateur naturalist who commissioned dozens of detailed views of Indian fauna, among them the sloe-eyed zebra at left. The sylvan scene opposite records the treetop antics of a family of squirrels. Jahangir's affection for his four-footed subjects purportedly led him to erect a hunting lodge in memory of a favorite deer.

A clever woman, Nur Mahal neither attempted to usurp power from Jahangir nor to contradict the few policies he thought fitting to promulgate. Instead, she delegated power through him until he became her puppet. Indeed, she understood her husband so well that she could inveigle him into any agreement — if it was late in the evening and if the emperor was drunk and amorous. During the later years of Jahangir's twenty-two-year reign, most imperial commands originated with Nur Mahal; in truth, she was the ruler of the Mogul Empire. At the same time, her power over the emperor did not prevent her from sharing his interests. She became as quick as he to recognize the subtleties of perspective and line in Persian paintings, as skilled as he at deciphering the hidden meanings in the poetry of the mystics. Together they composed couplets, although it was rumored that the queen had to restrain her poetic talents lest she outshine the World Seizer at his favorite hobby.

"If you marry a donkey," wrote a Persian proverbialist, "you must carry his load." And so it was for Nur Mahal. Jahangir became middle-aged and cantankerous, bitter for no other reason than the dull security of his uninspired reign. The last years of his life were passed in a struggle against senility, collapsing lungs, and delirium tremens. At the age of fifty-eight he died. Nur Mahal was banished to Lahore and there, in self-imposed seclusion, she ended her life directing the construction of Jahangir's beautiful tomb at Shahdara. Ironically, perhaps, his son and successor, Shah Jahan, was even then devoting much of his time and treasure to the construction and decoration of a grandiose monument of his own.

III

Monument to a Lasting Love

Tragedy, as we have seen, struck the fifth Mogul emperor, Shah Jahan, at the very outset of his reign. From the throne of the bereaved emperor to his grief-stricken court — and from the borders of India to foreign lands beyond — went the news that the "King of the World" was searching for an architect to design a magnificent tomb to hold the remains of his beloved wife, Mumtaz Mahal. From South India, from Burma, Egypt, Ceylon, from Transcaucasia and Persia came draftsmen anxious to please the emperor with their designs. Each day new arrivals presented themselves before His Majesty in the Red Fort at Agra. The monarch examined their drawings and, with an appropriate compliment or word of contempt, rejected them all.

And then to the court of Shah Jahan came the Turk Ustad Isa. Legend has it that he too had suffered the premature loss of his wife, and that he too was searching for a way in which his passion for a woman could be immortalized. The Turk displayed his drawings to Shah Jahan, who felt that they embodied all the qualities such a monument should possess. Next, a small wooden model was made. It met with immediate royal approval, and construction of the tomb began. For twenty-two years, 20,000 men and women labored night and day to give form to the emperor's majestic vision, and when they finished Shah Jahan was overwhelmed with the magnificence of what they had accomplished — so overwhelmed that to demonstrate his approval he chopped off the hands of the master builders, blinded the calligraphers, and cut off the architect's head so that none of these people could build an edifice to rival the Taj Mahal.

That, at least, is the legend. In reality we know almost nothing about the architect who designed the Taj Mahal and little of the men who raised it. "They were giants who built this cathedral," said Rodin of the Gothic church in Strasbourg, and it is true as well of the architect of the Taj. Such a man must have been remarkable, one of the great geniuses of all time. Yet it is as if his name had been amputated, not unlike the head of the architect in the legend, by the emperor's own chroniclers. What manner of man was he? And what was his name? The answer is that the Taj Mahal was designed by an Italian, a Venetian goldsmith named Geronimo Veroneo — or so we are informed by Father Sebastien Manrique.

Father Manrique was an Augustinian monk who came to the East in 1628 and settled in the Portuguese colony of Goa on India's southwestern coast. In 1642 he traveled to Agra in order to negotiate for the release of a certain Father Anthony, who had been taken hostage by the Moguls. Father Manrique apparently found his diplomatic duties in the capital undemanding, for he ended up spending twenty-six days touring the local sights. Near the banks of the Jumna River, on a grassy meadow facing the Red Fort, a tomb was being erected, one which so impressed Father Manrique that he decided to learn of its authors. His research turned up the following information:

> The architect of these works was a Venetian, by name Geronimo Veroneo, who had come to this part in a Portuguese ship and died in the city of Lahore before he reached it. . . . Fame, the swift conveyor of good and evil news, had spread the story that the Emperor summoned him and informed him that he desired to erect a great and sumptuous tomb for his dead wife,

and he was required to erect a great design for this, for the Emperor's inspection. The architect Veroneo carried out this order and within a few days proved the great skill he had in his way of procuring several models of the most beautiful architecture. He pleased the ruler in respect of his designs, but in his barbaric pride and arrogance, His Majesty was displeased with him owing to his low estimates, and it is said that, becoming very angry, he told Veroneo to spend three croires of rupees, that is three hundred lakhs, and to inform him when it was expended.

During the reign of Jahangir, a goldsmith named Veroneo did in fact come to India and, as mentioned by Father Manrique, did die on his way to Lahore. While in India, Veroneo lived for a time in Agra and must have prospered there, for he is reported to have provided a large sum of ransom money to free Portuguese captives imprisoned by the Moguls. He knew many influential Europeans throughout the North Indian provinces, and when he died, he was buried in the Christian cemetery of Padres Santos in Agra.

The theory that Veroneo designed the Taj Mahal is intriguing and it still finds occasional champions, especially, as one might suspect, in Italy. But the scales of evidence weigh heavily against it. True there is the testimony of Father Manrique, but he was really no more than a casual tourist who *heard* that the Taj Mahal had been built by an Italian. There are many facts to contradict his assertion. Nowhere else is mention made of Veroneo's participation in planning the Taj Mahal. As a matter of fact, there is no record that Veroneo had any skill other than that of working gold. Other Europeans who saw the Taj under construction

never mentioned his name, and furthermore, it is difficult to suppose that an artist trained in seventeenth-century Italy, the Italy of Bernini, could build a mausoleum that would not only typify Indo-Persian architecture but would become the symbol, par excellence, of the Eastern world. If a European architect had designed the building, would he not have left one fingerprint behind, one Greek cross or Doric column, one Biblical fresco or pink-cheeked *putto*? It is difficult to believe that he would not, for even transcendent genius is still in some ways bound to the cultural idiom of the society that produces it.

It should also be pointed out that Mumtaz Mahal was an archenemy of Christianity. Since the sixteenth century, Portuguese Christians had been migrating to Hooghly, a trading settlement on the northeast coast of India, near modern Calcutta. Although they practiced piracy and furthered the slave trade, the punishment scarcely fit the crime when Shah Jahan, goaded by his queen, ordered his soldiers to raze the entire colony. This they did with ghastly efficiency, destroying the Portuguese fleet and all its men along with a boatload of women and children, who disappeared into the black waters while their Jesuit leader, Father Frahlo, held a crucifix aloft. Four thousand prisoners were taken that day and marched from Hooghly to Agra, a distance of 1,200 miles. Those who survived were brutally disposed of; the priests were thrown beneath elephants and the rest were sold as slaves.

The instigator of this "holy" war was Mumtaz Mahal, whose sarcophagus bears an inscription immortalizing her hatred of infidels: "Lord defend us from the tribe of unbelievers." It is thus difficult to believe that the

These modern views — of water buffalo, a solitary boatman, and lush watermelon fields — reveal that life on the Jumna River has hardly changed in the three hundred years since the Taj Mahal was built on a platform overlooking Agra's muddy stream.

emperor, who was likewise antagonistic toward Christianity, would choose one of that faith to design the tomb of his most pious wife. Indeed, up to the time of the British occupation of India, any non-Moslem trespasser who entered the Taj was put to the sword.

If evidence for Geronimo Veroneo as author of the Taj is scanty, there is even less to support the claims of the French silversmith Austin de Bordeaux. This theory originated with an Englishman, Major Sleeman, who arrived in Agra in 1844 and fulfilled his dream of touring the Mogul monuments. In the book that invariably followed such excursions, he informs us that "the magnificent building [the Taj Mahal] and all the palaces of Agra and Delhi were, I believe, designed by Austin de Bordeaux, a Frenchman of great talent and merit, in whose ability and integrity the Emperor placed much reliance."

It is not difficult to see how Sleeman acquired this information. A Frenchman named Bordeaux did at one time live in India and was in fact a silversmith who had come to the East under dubious circumstances (it is said that he passed bogus gems in France). In the early part of the seventeenth century he traveled to Hindustan, where he found employment in the ateliers of Jahangir and, being a talented setter of stones, he had no trouble making a reputation. Bordeaux married an Indian woman, had one son, and when Jahangir died, stayed on as thronemaker to Shah Jahan. He was, however, a Christian like Veroneo, and like Veroneo his name is never linked in contemporary Mogul histories with the Taj. Furthermore, Bordeaux's claim to immortality is completely demolished by one of his own letters, now in the Bibliothèque Nationale

58

in Paris, in which the French silversmith admits a complete ignorance of draftsmanship and a total disinterest in architectural design.

When Bordeaux died, however, his name seems to have remained and somehow drifted down through the generations until it reached the ears of Sleeman. Perhaps it was brought to the major's attention by one of the "experts" or "guides" who have for centuries accosted tourists at the gateway of the queen's mausoleum; they may have kept the Frenchman's name in reserve for Europeans in general and for the British in particular, for in that period of their world dominion the latter were eager to trace all art of the world back to Western origins.

What then of the wandering Turk, Ustad Isa? He seems to belong almost wholly to the realm of the fantastic. To begin with, he had a number of aliases: Ustad Khan Effendi, Isa Mohammed Effendi, Ustad Mohammed, Isa Affendi, Isa Khan, and any number of permutations of the name. He is also said to have come from Constantinople, from Shiraz or Isfahan in Persia, from Samarqand in Bukhara, from Qandahar in Afghanistan, and even from Agra or Delhi. He is said to have been a Christian, an Arab, a Jew, a Russian, a Hindu, and even a Moslem fakir. Moreover, his name does not even appear until the beginning of the nineteenth century. And when it does — as if it had been a byword in Indian history for centuries — it shows up in almost every tourist handbook and schedule, just in time to satisfy the curiosity of the English travelers then journeying to Agra. Ustad Isa is probably a fictitious amalgam of Moslem-sounding names, most likely the invention of latter-day British guidebook writers.

A more plausible possible architect of the Taj Mahal is Ahmad, a Persian engineer-astrologer who frequently directed the emperor's most ambitious architectural projects — more plausible because he is specifically mentioned as the designer of the mausoleum in a manuscript written by his son. Yet, although Ahmad is a tantalizing possibility, almost nothing more is known of him or his activities. It must also be said that Mogul family histories were notoriously concerned with the glorification of their lineage, even at the price of prevarication. And in India, where the father is considered sacred, a son may write any sort of boast concerning his progenitor provided it adds to the latter's patriarchal glory. This may have been the case with the document written by Ahmad's son. Nor can we assume that because the attribution is contemporary, it is correct. There is, for instance, the case of Ali Mardan Khan, one of the great engineers and statesmen in the court of Shah Jahan, a man who is mentioned in a contemporary document as the designer of the dome of the Taj Mahal but who, it is also recorded, did not arrive in Agra until 1638, six years after construction of the dome had begun.

If we do not know the truth about the architect — or, more likely, architects — of the Taj Mahal, we are fortunately better informed about the artisans who constructed it. Long before the days of Shah Jahan, Indians had been famous throughout the Eastern world for their skill in working stone. During the eleventh century an Arabian historian named Alberuni, having heard reports of these draftsmen that bordered on the miraculous, traveled to India in order to witness their work firsthand. He was not disappointed. He found the Hindustanis particularly noteworthy in the construction of stone tanks, pools, and fountains. "In this," he wrote, "they have attained to a very high degree of art, so that our people when they see them, wonder at them, and are unable to describe them much less to construct anything like them."

Talks of these masters of brick and stone had long attracted the attention of various warlike neighbors; invading pre-Mogul India, these plunderers singled out the best of the Hindustani artists and brought them home to beautify their own cities. One such conqueror was Timur, always a great enthusiast of the arts, equally as ready to annihilate the population of a province as he was to gently succor its artists and bring them to his capital city, Samarqand. There these wards became the pride of his marble workshops, and when the awesome Turk died they helped build his tomb, the Guri Amir — significantly, one of the models on which the Taj Mahal was later based. Centuries after Timur's death, when Akbar lured artists to his benign patronage and Jahangir pampered them like children, the descendants of the artists carried away to the north returned to India. By the time Shah Jahan commenced work on the Taj, his ateliers were crowded with the most able engineers, carvers, and stonemasons who could be found throughout the East.

Despite such a brilliant labor force, a project as ambitious as the tomb of Mumtaz Mahal demanded talent from many quarters. In 1632, as construction of the queen's mausoleum began, artists from across Asia converged on Agra, making it one of the most vital creative centers on earth for the next twenty years. The names of these foreign workers have been recorded; and if the records are accurate, the Taj Mahal was indeed one of the most eclectic creations of all time. From Turkey came Ismail Afandi, a designer of hemispheres and a builder of domes, a man no doubt put to this task by his previous Ottoman masters, who, like many other Moslems, considered the dome to be the most perfect of all terrestrial forms. Qazim Khan, a native of Lahore and a renowned worker of precious metals, traveled to the capital of Shah Jahan to cast the solid gold finial that would crown the Turkish master's dome. A local lapidary from Delhi, Chiranji Lal, was chosen as chief mosaicist, a special distinction. Invented in Persia before the time of Christ and brought to the West via Greece and Italy, mosaic work became popular in Moslem India during the eighth and ninth centuries. It became a fundamental element in tomb and mosque design, and the art was perfected by the Mogul inlayers who set scrolls and flourishes with such dexterity that legend claims they could see through stone and cut gems with their eyes.

To oversee finances and the management of daily production, the emperor chose two seasoned administrators, Mir Abdul Karim and Mukarrimat Khan of Shiraz. Mir Abdul Karim was especially experienced. He had served Jahangir for many years, acting as supervisor for many of the emperor's pet schemes. "As I have decided to go to the Deccan," Jahangir wrote in his memoirs, "I have ordered Abdul Karim to go to Mandu and prepare a novel house for my private residence and restore the buildings of the ancient kings." Before Jahangir died, he rewarded Mir Abdul Karim with four hundred horses, eight hundred slaves, and the inevitable string of honorific titles. The second superinten-

dent, Mukarrimat Khan of Shiraz, had also served Jahangir, and he too had been granted honors. A Persian from the city of Shiraz, he was one of the numerous Safawid workmen connected with the Taj Mahal. Superior in certain respects to their Mogul peers in learning and methodology, Persian administrators and artists were consequently imported to India in large numbers, with the result that the style of the Taj Mahal — as well as that of practically every other major building the Moguls erected — is as Persian as it is Hindustani.

From Shiraz also came the master calligrapher Amanat Khan, who was given the task of adorning the façade and burial chamber with Arabic lettering. As early as the seventh century, calligraphic inscription had been a primary characteristic of Moslem architecture. It appeared in niches, above doorways, on minarets, inside domes and spandrels, practically everywhere, serving not only as a means of displaying scriptural verses, not only as an ingenious embellishment, but also as one of the essential elements in the delineation of architectonic space. A calligrapher was thus of such importance that he was ranked with the architect himself, and Amanat Khan was apparently worthy of this rank. Not only did he receive his share of slaves and noble titles (he was also the master calligrapher for Akbar's tomb), but his was the only signature thought worthy to be written on the walls of the Taj. It is located at the base of the interior dome near lines from the Koran, and it reads: "Written by the insignificant being, Amanat Khan Shirazi."

Accompanying this international assemblage of artificers were others who brought with them fine and diverse skills. Two additional calligraphers, Mohammed Khan of Baghdad and Roshan Khan of Syria, were imported to Agra, and with them came the Arabian Kadir Zeman Khan, who billed himself as a master of all the arts. Joining this factotum was a Baluchistani stonecutter named Amir Ali, a mason from Balkh, and an engineer from Samarqand, the latter two being perhaps descendants of the stoneworkers kidnapped by Timur three centuries earlier. Sculptors from Bukhara, calligraphers from Persia, inlayers from South India, a man who specialized in building turrets, another who carved only marble flowers — thirty-seven men in all formed the creative nucleus, and to this core was added a labor force of twenty thousand workers recruited from across North India.

Twenty thousand men and women constitute a city, and a small city did indeed arise outside Agra. Situated in the courtyard beyond the Taj, it was known first as Tasimacan, "A great bazaar or marketplace, composed of six courts all encompassed with porticos under which there are warehouses for merchants." As the settlement grew in size and importance, it was renamed Mumtazabad after the dead queen. Many caravans en route to Agra stopped at Mumtazabad, and the little metropolis at times knew greater prosperity than its larger neighbor — indeed, its prosperity was bolstered by Shah Jahan's endowment, the revenues taken from thirty neighboring villages. The emperor, it seems, even considered moving all of official Agra to this locale, in the manner that Akbar had once brought his court to Fatehpur Sikri. "He intends, as some think," wrote a traveler, "to remove all the cittie hither, causeinge hills to be made levell because they might

hinder the prospect of it, places appoynted for streets, shoppes, etc. dwellings, commanding Merchants, shopkeepers, Artificers to Inhabit it where they begin to repaire. . . ." Plans for this ambitious transfer never materialized, however, and forty years later the bazaars of Mumtazabad were as silent as those of Fatehpur Sikri.

Along with the laborers flocking to Agra, materials for construction also began arriving: principally red sandstone from local quarries and marble dug from the hills of far-off Makran. Although the treasury was well-filled, such prodigious quantities of rare stuffs were now required that caravans traveled to all corners of the empire and beyond in search of precious materials. From China came jade and crystal; from Tibet, turquoise; from Afghanistan, lapis lazuli; from Egypt, chrysolite; from the Indian Ocean, rare shells, coral, and mother-of-pearl. Topazes, onyxes, garnets, sapphires, bloodstones, forty-three different types of gems in all — ranging in rarity from Himalayan quartz to Golconda diamonds — were ultimately to be used in embellishing the Taj Mahal.

Late in 1631, the body of the queen was brought to Agra from Burhanpur and placed beneath a temporary dome near the proposed site of the tomb. Construction started almost immediately. First an area larger than three football fields was excavated and filled with sediment to avoid seepage from the Jumna River, which had recently been diverted to the foot of the foundation in order to improve the vista from the completed tomb. An enormous scaffolding was set up; for reasons never understood, it was built of brick rather than the traditional bamboo. So colossal was this scaffolding

said to be that when the mausoleum was completed and the time came to dismantle it, experts informed the emperor that it would take five years to remove it. Shah Jahan pondered the question carefully, and finally had it announced that all peasants who helped dismantle the structure could keep the bricks they removed. The scaffolding came down in a single day — or so, at least, says another popular legend.

In order to transport materials, a ten-mile-long ramp of tamped earth was built through Agra, and on it trudged an unending parade of elephants and bullock carts dragging blocks of marble to the building site. During his stay in Agra, Father Manrique was witness to these labors:

> [Blocks of white marble] had been brought there from over forty leagues away for the erection of these edifices. Some of these blocks, which I met on the way when visiting Biana City, were of such unusual size and length that they drew the sweat of many powerful teams of oxen and of fierce-looking, big-horned buffaloes, which were dragging enormous, strongly-made wagons, in teams of twenty or thirty animals.

Once the marble reached the Taj, it was hoisted into place by means of an elaborate post-and-beam pulley manned by teams of mules and masses of workers tugging and hauling in the supposed manner of the Egyptian pyramid builders. The first buildings to be constructed were the tomb proper and the two mosques that flank it; then came the four minarets; finally the gateway and auxiliary buildings were erected. All were built as integral parts of a single unit, carefully planned to harmonize, for a law of Islam decrees that once a tomb is completed nothing can ever be added to it and absolutely nothing can ever be taken away from it.

As the Taj Mahal slowly rose from the banks of the Jumna, Shah Jahan was often there to oversee its growth. Each year he held a solemn memorial service on the grounds; and when the tomb was at last completed, a sheet of pearls was spread over the coffin and a solid gold balustrade was placed around it. The emperor chose his finest diamonds and set them on the casket. He sent holy men to pray beside the sarcophagus and dispatched two thousand soldiers to guard the grounds. The floors of the interior chamber, today empty and worn smooth by the passing of many feet (one can only enter the Taj barefoot or with special canvas slippers) were covered with the best carpets from Persian and Mogul looms, and these were changed several times a week. A door of solid jasper was placed in one of the inner passageways; silver candlesticks and gold lamps were attached to the walls; gates of solid silver graced the entranceway; and a delicate incense perfumed the air. Today none but the delicate incense remains; all the other treasures were carried away to unknown places by the multitude of plunderers who came to North India in the days after the Mogul sun had passed its zenith.

Illustrious visitors also came and went, some of them European. Father Manrique saw the Taj Mahal when it was almost completed — and no doubt justified his mild enthusiasm for the pagan sanctuary by rationalizing that it was, after all, the brainchild of a Western mind. Workers were then laying out the gardens, planting trees and flowers. Since Manrique reports that only one thousand men were on the job, we can assume that the year 1642 was one of relatively little activity.

Stark simplicity is the keynote of the geometric design (far left) on the lower platform of the Taj Mahal. Visitors must remove their shoes (left) before entering the tomb itself.

Two other Occidentals, a Frenchman named Jean Baptiste Tavernier and an Englishman named Peter Mundy, also visited Agra at the time the Taj was built. In 1632, Mundy mentions that "there is alreadye about her tombe a rail of gold," and he tells us that "the building is begun and goes on with excessive labour and cost prosecuted with extraordinary diligence, gold and silver, esteemed metal and marble. . . ." The merchant Tavernier goes into detail describing the Taj as it looked in 1654, immediately after completion, and it is from him that we learn the building was twenty-two years in the making. (This statistic is contradicted by an inscription above the gateway of the Taj which reads: "Completed by the grace of God on 1057 A.H. (1642 A.D.)," and by a number of other estimates which would have the date of completion fall anywhere between 1642 and 1654. Although it may never be known for certain, it is likely that the tomb itself took ten years to construct and the entire complex another twelve.) "I saw the beginning and compleating of this great work," Tavernier writes, "that cost two and twenty years labor, and twenty thousand men always at work."

Of those Westerners who saw the Taj Mahal when it was new, none was more impressed than another Frenchman, François Bernier, a physician at the court of Louis XIV who was singularly well-versed in matters architectural. During this period, Westerners considered much Eastern art to be curious and rather bizarre manifestations of a primitive mentality. To treat it with seriousness, let alone to compare it with those matchless productions of the Western spirit, was to invite certain ridicule. Nevertheless, Bernier was willing to chance such a comparison, and this ranks him as one of the first Europeans to admit openly the merits of Indian culture and to acknowledge the splendor of its finest monument:

The last time I visited the Tage Mahale's mausoleum, I was in the company of a French merchant [Tavernier], who, as well as myself, thought this extraordinary fabric could not be sufficiently admired. I did not venture to express my opinion, fearing that my taste might have become corrupted by my long residence in the *Indies*; and as my companion was come recently from *France* it was quite a relief to my mind to hear him say that he had seen nothing in *Europe* so bold and majestic.

IV

At the Great Mogul's Court

In the year 1631, twenty thousand laborers at Agra began quarrying and carving marble for the Taj Mahal. Thirty years later, on the other side of the planet, another prodigious labor force commenced work on a similarly grandiose project, the palace of Versailles. Its builder was Louis XIV, who had been crowned king of France in 1643, the midpoint of Shah Jahan's thirty-year reign. Like Shah Jahan, Louis XIV was a connoisseur of architecture on the grandest of scales. Like Jahan, he ruled for many years over a civilization that had reached the apogee of its magnificence, and like his Indian counterpart, Louis was the last great monarch in his line, a line that collapsed within a century of his death in a welter of bloodshed and internal decay. There are, in fact, so many parallels between these two resplendent sovereigns — a world apart, although near contemporaries — that a comparison is quite revealing.

Both Shah Jahan and Louis XIV had an almost organic need for excessive extravagance. Their clothing, their weapons, their baths, their beds, almost everything had to be leafed with gold, inlaid with onyx, fashioned by the finest artisans. Factories were built exclusively for the production of baubles for a king's titillation. Louis had his ruby perfume applicators, his three silver wig blocks, his emerald ear spoons. Shah Jahan possessed seven jeweled thrones, any one of which would have pleased the most ostentatious of monarchs elsewhere. The Mogul emperor once appeared in a coat so heavily studded with gems that two servants were required to keep him from collapsing; Louis, as if not to be outdone, once received the Siamese ambassador in the Hall of Mirrors stumbling

beneath the weight of his own glamorous garment, a fur robe encrusted with diamonds and valued at one-sixth the cost of Versailles itself.

Both courts reveled in protocol, which has rarely been carried to such extremes. The length of a sleeve, the height of a stool, an invitation to dinner, permission to wear gold brocade, such details determined the fortunes of French and Mogul subjects alike. In Agra, one never knocked at the chambers of a superior; one fell to the knees and tapped three times with the back of the hand. Similarly, to knock at a door at Versailles was gauche; instead one scratched with the little finger of the left hand, and for this purpose courtiers let that particular nail grow long. When watching the Sun King eat, a popular pastime, all spectators wore hats; it was considered disrespectful to display the top of one's head at a royal dinner. At the Red Fort, to exhibit the bottom of one's feet in the presence of the emperor was likewise an outrage and offenders were obliged to shave their heads immediately. Prestige in Louis's domain was measured by the height of the chair one was allowed to possess, and only the king and queen could sit in chairs with arms. At the Mogul court, chairs were also a symbol of prestige, so much so that to occupy one in the presence of the emperor was among the highest of royal rewards. In the corridors of Shah Jahan's palace, if the ruler's dinner happened to be carried by, the beholder had to throw himself face downward on the floor. At Versailles, in the same circumstances, etiquette ruled that a courtier must bow, remove his hat, and whisper in a voice filled with awe and respect, "The meat of the king."

Both men placed themselves on display. For a mem-

ber of the French bourgeoisie it was considered as great a day's outing to ride from Paris to Versailles and watch the king eat in public as it was for a citizen of Agra to walk each dawn to the courtyard of the Red Fort, where Shah Jahan sat for an hour exhibited on the public balcony.

Shah Jahan and Louis were both handsome men, as famous for their beauty as for the frequency of their romantic dalliances. In the more permissive world of the harem, Shah Jahan's concubines (five thousand of them) were legend. But if Louis was confined by Judeo-Christian propriety to take his mistresses one at a time, he chose them — to say the least — in close sequence. And as to the promiscuity of his court: "Is there in all the world another town where the husbands are as patient as here?" asked Molière.

Nevertheless, in spite of their numberless indiscretions, Louis and Shah Jahan were each basically dominated by one female figure. For Shah Jahan this figure was Mumtaz Mahal; for Louis it was his second wife, Madame de Maintenon. Both of these prepossessing women were also motivating forces behind religious persecutions. The extermination of the Christian Portuguese colony in Bengal was partly the work of Mumtaz Mahal; and in France, the revocation of the Edict of Nantes that forced so many French Protestants into exile was said to have been instigated by Madame de Maintenon.

These two seventeenth-century kings, both lovers of the hunt and of the arts and, above all, patrons of the elaborate monuments that they built — essentially to themselves — were the last chapters in the book of omnipotent monarchy, a chronicle that began in the West with the Roman emperors, in the East with the Chinese scholar-kings, and which ended in both when the British became imperialists and a deluge engulfed France. Yet magnificent as the French court was, with its baroque castles and month-long festivals at which ten thousand courtiers attended open-air plays written for the occasion by Molière and Racine, it was easily eclipsed by the court of the Great Mogul — as Shah Jahan was called in the West.

The court of the Great Mogul was situated in three locations; Delhi, Lahore, and Agra. Of his three principal residences, the Red Fort in Agra was the most impressive. Started by Akbar and completed by Shah Jahan, this walled complex of mosques, harems, gardens, and palaces was the pride of the Moguls. "Near the river also is the royal citadel [the Red Fort] which is the greatest and most magnificent in the Whole East," wrote a visitor to the Red Fort, "for it is almost four English miles in circumference and is everywhere surrounded by a wall of squared stone." The royal apartments were ornamented with ruby-encrusted arabesques and crowned with ceilings of solid gold. Musicians were kept performing continuously, even in empty rooms, on the chance that the emperor might pause for a moment's entertainment. In the imperial kitchens, fifteen complete meals were always ready to be served at a moment's notice by a unit of richly dressed kitchen slaves. Embroidered tapestries and choice Persian paintings, enamel lamps that burned scented oil, gold decanters filled with lemonade, a box of pearls, trays of guavas or mangoes, or grapes from Kashmir, pillows, carpets, mirrors, melons, silver goblets filled with night wine or lilacs, seven slender pillars

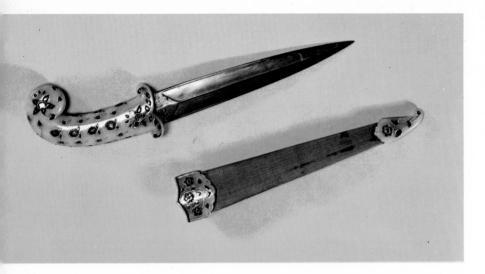

Mogul ostentation reached its apogee with Shah Jahan. To commemorate his own coronation, the fifth Mogul emperor commissioned the gem-studded Peacock Throne, which survives only in written descriptions and royal portraits (right). Lapidaries and goldsmiths thrived under Jahan's patronage. The pale jade hilt of the dagger at left is inlaid with gold, diamonds, emeralds, and rubies; on the well-honed blade is an inscription in gold wire; and even the velvet sheath is mounted with jewels and jade.

wrapped in satin drapery — all were here, the trimmings of an Arabian night's reverie. Meanwhile the emperor, the creator and *prima personna* of this garden of earthly delights, bathed with the harem in his underground pool, where the light of a thousand candles danced in the reflection of ten thousand mirrors and countless gems encrusted on the walls.

Each day of the week Shah Jahan ruled from a different throne. The greatest of these was the Takht-i-Taus, the Peacock Throne, which was built in 1628 to commemorate his coronation (and a poor copy of which today seats the shah of Iran). The Takht-i-Taus was perhaps the most lavish throne ever made in India. It took seven years to complete and cost a million rupees. Although the throne has been destroyed, descriptions of it still exist. The throne itself, we are told, consisted of an elevated rectangular platform on which twelve emerald-studded pillars were placed, the capitals of each composed of two jeweled peacocks standing on either side of a diamond-leafed tree. These pillars supported a canopy, six feet by four feet, which was covered with configurations of pearls, emeralds, sapphires, and gold. In order to mount the throne one climbed a staircase of solid silver. "But," wrote a poet much in favor with the emperor, "not because of its gems but because it kisses the feet of Shah Jahan, has the value of the throne ascended to heaven."

The raw materials for the construction of such glamorous follies were supplied by the seemingly limitless Mogul coffers. The treasury at Agra listed the following assets:

750 pounds of pearls, 275 pounds of emeralds, 5,000 gems from Cathay, corals, topazes, and other less precious stones in almost infinite number, 200 daggers, 1,000 gold studded saddles with jewels, 2 golden thrones, 3 silver thrones, 100 silver chairs, 5 golden chairs, 200 most precious mirrors, 100,000 precious silver plates and utensils, 50,000 pounds of gold plate, wrought gold and silver, Chinese vessels, worked necklaces, cups, discs, candelabra, tubs of uncut diamonds, gold images of elephants, golden bridals, porcelain vessels. . . .

Nor did this depository of riches comprise the complete fortune of Baber's descendants; the treasure house in Lahore was said to contain more than three times as much royal booty.

Perhaps no other civilization has ever put its wealth to such conspicuously self-indulgent ends. What is surprising is that in India, as in seventeenth-century France, an intense religious life existed side-by-side with the life of the senses, and any man of that day, no matter how involved in his own physical gratifications, was inevitably devout. Lines of demarcation between the sacred and profane were vague, so convinced were all men that the world-apparent was unreal, a shadow dance behind which stood a divine absolute. It was believed that all activities could serve as substance for religious development, provided a man remembered God during his involvements, no matter how base these involvements might be. Indeed, the God who stood behind material appearances could be reached by incessant meditation and remembrance even if this remembrance occurred while one was sipping wine in a garden or leading an elephant brigade to war.

Thus the emperor, following conferences on matters of war and diplomacy, might retire to the company of

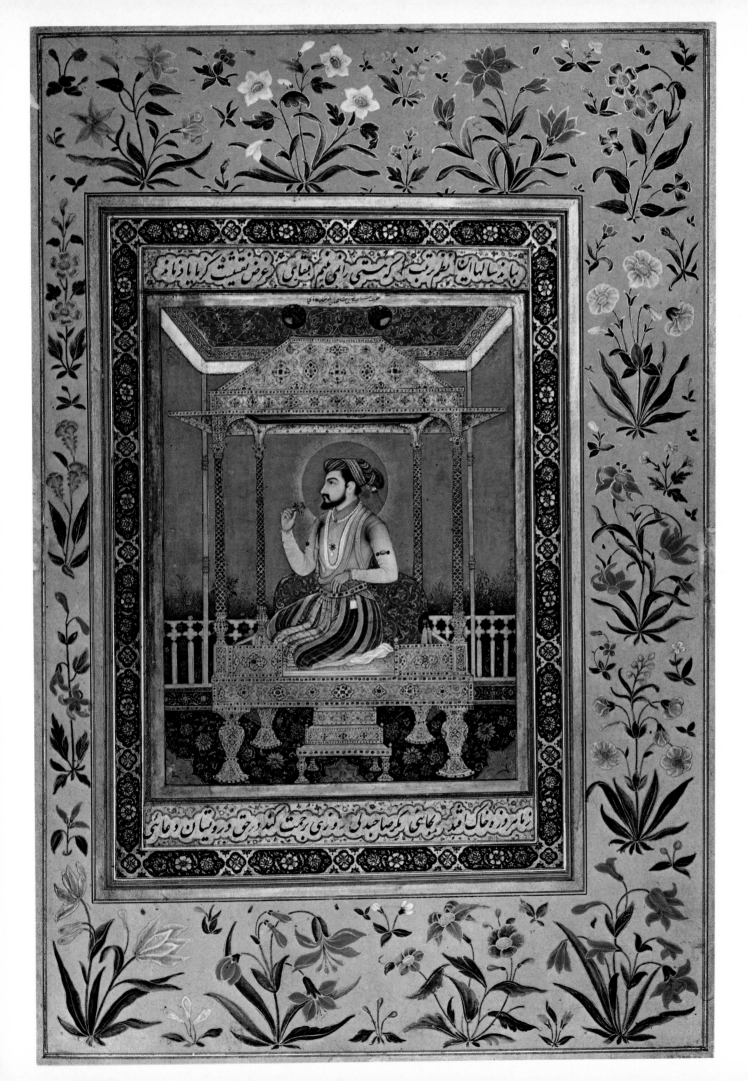

The Hindu population in Mogul India suffered under alternately tolerant and tyrannical decrees while Moslem mystics known as Sufis (left) enjoyed unusual freedom. The youthful Shah Jahan (right) was himself educated by Sufi tutors.

learned holy men and pass the evening in theological discourse. In the mirror-studded bath and in the passageways of subterranean dungeons, candles burned continually for God, and engraved on every wineglass and opium pipe was the name of Allah. Soldiers who slaughtered ten men in battle might pass the night praying for the men they had slain; on the jade hilts of their razor-sharp scimitars were inscribed verses from the Koran. Poetry dealt with worldly and ribald themes, yet between the lines a complex allegorical symbolism spoke of the yearning of the soul for the Divine. All songs, all music, all art, drama and literature was essentially devotional, and even the performances of puppet shows or traveling minstrels were based on ancient tradition. Every aspect of life was governed by religious law. The most temporal pursuits, such as hunting or closing a business transaction, were overseen by iron-clad attendance to the Moslem code, and the simple acts of greeting a relative or washing the hands with pea flour were maintained by protocol taken from religious custom or directly from the Koran.

The Sufis, who were Moslem mystics, had the last of their golden days in India at this time, and much of the best Mogul science and literature was the product of their talents. Deeply involved in art and life, the Sufis were mysterious men, entirely lacking in dogma and hard to pin down as to their actual beliefs. Akin in spirit to the anonymous artists who built the Gothic churches of Europe, they appeared abruptly to do their good works and vanished just as quickly, using their obscurity as a means to work unbothered by the praise and scorn of the uninitiated. Even the Mogul rulers, often educated by Sufis in the same way Chinese emperors

were tutored by Zen monks, rarely tried to tinker with their designs. These devout men could be found anywhere. They often took part in everyday life, and unknown to the populace, worked at ordinary affairs, as shopkeepers or calligraphers, sometimes having large families and many wives. Occasionally they also took part in the world of the palace, where they were welcomed and where they can still be seen in paintings of the day, standing by the emperor in positions ordinarily reserved for the highest ranking lords.

Complementing religion's universal reign was the populace's unquestioning belief in the efficacy of the supernatural. Magic was a standard ingredient in the diet of all men. No activity was too trifling, no decision too insignificant to be carried out without the advice of an astrologer. The resolution to purchase a slave or add hunting dogs to the pack was first checked against the *sahet,* the exactly appropriate moment for any transaction or event. Marriages, military alliances, partnerships, undertakings of every account were commenced only with knowledge of the astrologically auspicious moment. In addition, curses, witchcraft, and black magic had been used for centuries in India. The sight of a painted fakir muttering incantations before a skull and ritual instrument was a common one, and few people had to guess at the meaning of such a ceremony — someone had been wronged, someone would be punished. Conjurers of all degrees of accomplishment flourished, furnishing credulous European visitors with stories of the rope trick and disappearing hands. Tavernier saw one such stunt: before his eyes a twig was made to grow into a blossoming tree with no other soil than the magician's own blood. Bernier too, if a bit

dubiously, tells that he heard of such things, of men who could read any man's thoughts or could hatch a bird from an egg held on the breast.

Today, wandering through the ruins of mosques or studying the contours of mausoleum domes that shimmer in uncertain outline behind waves of heat, one still feels that the Indian landscape is saturated in mysticism. Here, in a world called illusory, in a world moving in half time, as if underwater, in a world of flies and sand and countless transformations, where gypsies camp in Mogul rubble and children stare into the sun, men move through the heat of their sad days, sensing all life as significant, capable of subtle influence simply because it is there.

In such an atmosphere, Shah Jahan had been raised and had grown to manhood. He was born, according to the most reliable data, on January 5, 1592, in the city of Lahore. It was a magnificent place, described by a European traveler who saw it then as "the goodly city of Lahore in India, one of the largest cities of the whole universe. For it containest at least XVI miles in compass and exceedeth Constantinople in size and greatness." The mother of the future emperor was a Rajput princess, Manmati, and his father, Jahangir, had been half Hindu, making him only one-fourth Moslem. Nonetheless, he soon turned his back on the Rajput heritage, becoming a strict and often intolerant Sunni Moslem. His name as a prince, Khurram, meant "Joyous." It had been chosen by Akbar, who sometimes allowed his grandson to accompany him on foreign military campaigns where, in the midst of battle, he gave the fledgling prince first-hand lessons in the arts of war. When the great monarch lay dying, his young

grandson was by the bedside. Told to go into the adjoining room, Khurram replied: "So long as there is a breath of life in Shah Baba [Akbar], nothing can induce me to leave him."

The prince received a well-rounded education designed to train not only his mind but, in conformity with the ancient model of the total man, his heart and hands as well. His favorite teachers were Sufis. He was instructed in science and medicine by one Hakim Ali Gilan; in later life Shah Jahan remembered this sage as the wisest man he had ever known. From other Sufis he learned grammar, logic, mathematics, astronomy, and geology, all sophisticated disciplines of the day. Pundits instructed him in Arabic, the language of the Koran, and in Persian. The latter was especially important in Mogul society, for it was the language of all official documents and was spoken and written by the Moguls up until the eighteenth century. Prince Khurram participated in sports with great aptitude and became an excellent rider and swordsman. In accordance with Islamic custom, he also received daily instruction in spiritual studies, and wrote the Koran over and over so many times that — as was expected of devout Moslems — he gradually committed most of the book to memory.

He grew up to be the most handsome of all Mogul kings. Portraits of him delineate an aristocratic nose, a high forehead, and languid eyes far less Mongol than those of his father. As a child, Shah Jahan had been scarred by smallpox; although the scars fail to appear in his portraits for obvious reasons, they perhaps explain why he was the first Mogul ruler to wear a beard.

As emperor, Shah Jahan had neither the energy of Baber nor the genius of Akbar, but he was nevertheless

Predictably, many artworks produced during Shah
Jahan's reign were portrayals of the emperor. On
the luminous enameled cameo at right, above, he
appears in the heroic guise of a lion slayer. In
the unusual double-page illumination below, Shah
Jahan accepts a gift of pearls from Asaf Khan, his
chief minister (right), while admiring courtiers
look on (left). The miniature at right of a gentle
poet seated in a cherry-blossom garden is proof that
even nonroyal themes were exquisitely executed.

an extremely capable administrator, careful and thorough in everything he attempted. "He never leaves today's business for tomorrow," said one of his court historians, "and no business before him suffers delay." A description of a single day in his life bears out the historian's observation.

At four o'clock Shah Jahan rose, turned west toward Mecca, and recited morning prayers. He then dressed with the aid of innumerable slaves, each appointed to deliver a particular article of clothing in the way Louis XIV had courtiers at his bedside appointed to similar tasks. After his jewels arrived from their nightly keep in the harem, he proceeded to the mosque, where for two hours he would kneel in prayer. Then he returned to the palace and, as the sun rose, stepped out onto a marble balcony. Throngs of people would jockey and push for a glimpse of the royal countenance. There would be heated shouts of *"Padshah salamat"* ("Long live the king"). If he were in a good mood, he would hear petitions from peasants, complaints from landlords, appeals for clemency from criminals. After an hour of this, it was time to move on, perhaps to the Jasmine Pavilion where he would be able to enjoy his favorite spectacle, an elephant fight.

Only a king could order an elephant fight. It was a time-honored royal prerogative. Elephants were brought from Sumatra and Siam, where they were chosen for their fierceness in the way bulls are picked for the ring in Spain today. The men who rode these fighting pachyderms were highly trained for the purpose. But unlike the elephants, who ordinarily lived to fight another day, their riders considered themselves fortunate if they escaped with only the loss of a limb,

and before each fight they took leave of their families as if under penalty of death. The combat would be considered finished when one elephant dominated another and brought it to the ground. Then they were separated by a *charkhi,* a hollow bamboo cross with gun powder in each end that whirled like a pinwheel when ignited and frightened the animals from their deadly embrace.

When the elephant fights were finished, the emperor walked in procession to the Diwan-i-Am, the Hall of Public Audience, where he sat at the Holy Window and conducted the morning's business. Behind him were servants swatting flies with yak-tail whisks and guards with banners displaying the Mogul insignia, a lion couchant in front of a rising sun. On either side were members of the royal family. Below them stood Asaf Khan, prime minister and the father of Mumtaz Mahal, and one step down, separated from royalty by balustrades, were throngs of courtiers, sultans, governors, men of state, each carefully positioned in order of rank and each standing with his head bowed before the Great Mogul.

The business of the day at last began. The emperor dispatched orders to the provinces, made suggestions for pensions and promotions, appropriated funds, examined requests for charity, dictated letters and signed them with his palm print, and heard the appeals of trembling supplicants, some of whom might be kept standing for hours until Shah Jahan looked up and asked after their demands. While these proceedings took place, musicians played — music so soft and sweet that it reportedly never took one's mind off the business of the day.

Indian noblemen maintained harems commensurate with their means and station. The prince at right appears content with the pleasures possible in his somewhat modest entourage.

Executive affairs concluded, Shah Jahan rested. Rare gifts sent by friendly neighbors or taken from vanquished enemies might be examined. Exotic animals, among them rhinoceros and anteaters, were paraded along the riverbank. An exhibit of elephants would be presented, and as each animal passed the emperor, it was prompted to fall on its knees and trumpet a salute. The elephants' feed — meal, wheat, and sugar cane — was always placed on display. This was done to keep the indigent handlers honest; otherwise they might have eaten the food themselves.

At eleven-thirty the emperor moved to a private tower, the Shah Burj, where in the company of his sons and trusted viceroys he reviewed confidential matters. In these private rooms stood Asaf Khan gazing with shrewd eyes at the pious and strangely aloof prince Aurangzeb. Here was the empty-headed prince Murad, a gullible brute, ready to tip a cup or go to war at the slightest provocation. Here was the emperor himself, engaged in hushed conversation with his best friend, Afzal Khan, while nearby the engineer Ali Mardan Khan and the royal physician, Wazir Khan, spoke of the campaigns in Assam or of the emperor's latest madness, a two-hundred-mile-long canal in the Punjab. Here agreements were made and agreements broken with rapidity, as the most powerful men in India came face-to-face each morning to play manipulation politics. Behind these doors the history of the empire was really made. After the private conference, more prayers were recited, followed by more business, this time in the Hall of Public Audience. Then it was time to eat. A team of Tatars tasted each of Shah Jahan's dishes to be sure they had not been poisoned, and the meal was served.

The emperor ate lightly and upon finishing went to the harem.

To comprehend the mentality of the Moguls it is advisable to pause and examine that complex institution, the harem. Western daydreams aside, the appeasement of the royal sexual appetite was but a small part of the harem's function. In a general sense, the harem was simply the place where women lived; it was the women's quarters. Babies were born there and children grew up there. Within it were markets, bazaars, laundries, kitchens, storage bins, playgrounds, schools, baths, all the facilities necessary to maintain a large household. The treasury was also kept there, as were secret documents and state seals. It served as a quiet spot where the emperor could work on business matters undisturbed, and it was the place where he sometimes slept at night. The harem was a typical domestic organization, a private household on a grand scale, existing not only to house the imperial ladies but to protect them from the gaze and molestations of an outside world where all unaccompanied and unveiled women were, ipso facto, prostitutes.

Like any large organization, the harem had a hierarchy. Its chief authorities were the wives and relatives of the emperor. Below them were thousands of lesser ladies, ranging from concubines to scullery slaves, and so large were the confines of this city of women that the lowest of these slaves might never lay eyes on the emperor himself.

The harem was guarded by three lines of defense. The first were Tatar women, Uzbegs, with whom "in comparison the Amazons were soft and timorous." We know little about these strange women who were sup-

posedly brought from secret valleys in Turkestan, but it seems from all reports that they were indeed of gargantuan proportions, stronger than most men, and deadly with spear and bow.

Next came the eunuchs, whose job it was to maintain discipline within the harem. The eunuchs were an exotic lot, a mixture of Asian and African types, some recruited as children from local districts, some received as gifts from Turkish and North African kings. Besides being skilled at controlling the wards of the harem, an accomplished eunuch could be invaluable to his master. But for this the accuracy of his judgments of men had to be impeccable; he had to be expert at gathering news of the courts and slow to repeat it to any but his master; he had to be loyal in the face of all change; and especially, he had to be keen with his political advice. If he were all these things, he might then gain great power within the household and even in the government, where he could sometimes rise to a position of high departmental authority. Between a ruler and his favorite eunuch a great friendship occasionally arose — the eunuch was often the only person a sovereign felt he could trust — and in Agra there were even a few lofty mausoleums built for these "men less than men" who had won royal favor.

The third and last line of harem defenders was stationed outside the walls. These were rugged male foot soldiers, equipped with rifles and ordered to open fire on any suspicious intruder. There are many stories of these brutal custodians tossing men off high walls or boiling them in oil, and it is certain that with these and other lines of protection the sanctity of the harem was rarely violated.

Inside the harem, life was absurdly luxurious. Every morning new fabrics arrived for the royal ladies. They were worn once and once only and then given away to slaves. Women amused themselves with an assortment of entertainments or lay quietly in open-air pavilions watching carp with gold rings in their noses swim in marble fountains. Fireworks, gazelle fights, pigeon flying, wrestling matches, acrobats, card games, musicians, archery, dancing bears, snake charmers, storytelling, all were part of the day's diversions. Yet, as might be supposed, the psychology of the harem woman, confined to her gilded prison, was often perverse. Jealousies and petty hatreds abounded, were endemic in fact, and competition for the attentions of the emperor often led to hideous crimes. Francis Pelsaert, a European who visited Jahangir, has left us this description:

All live together in their enclosure surrounded by high walls which is called the Mahal, having tanks and gardens inside. Each wife had apartments for herself and her slaves of which there may be 10 or 20 or 100, according to her fortunes. Each has a regular monthly allowance for her expenditures. Jewels and clothes are provided by the husband according to the extent of his affection. Their food comes from one kitchen, but each wife takes it in her own apartments, for they hate each other secretly, though they seldom or never allow it to be seen, because of their desire to retain the favors of their husband whom they fear, honor and worship as a god rather than as a man. Each night he visits a particular wife, or Mahal, and receives a very warm welcome from her and from the slaves, who dressed especially for the occasion, seem to fly rather than run, about their duties. If it is the hot weather they undress the husband as soon as he arrives and rub his body with pounded sandlewood and rose water, or some other scented or cooling oil. Fans are kept going steadily in the room, or in the open air, where they usually sit. Some of the slaves chafe the master's hands and feet, some sit and sing or play music and dance or provide other recreation, the wife sitting near all the time. They study day and night how to make exciting perfumes, such as *mosseri* or *falonj,* containing amber, pearls, gold and opium and other stimulants; but they are mostly for their own use, for they eat them occasionally in the day-time because they produce a pleasant elevation of the spirit. In the cool of the evening they drink a good deal of wine, for the women learn the habit quickly from their husbands, and drinking has become very fashionable in the last few years. The husband sits like a golden cock among his hens until midnight or until passion or drink sends him to bed. Then if one of the pretty slave girls takes his fancy, he calls her and enjoys her, his wife not daring to show any signs of displeasure, but dissembling, though she will take it out on the slave-girl later.

On a typical day, Shah Jahan would have left the harem at three o'clock, said his afternoon prayers, and seated himself in the Hall of Private Audience, where final statements would be delivered and letters dictated to scribes. Conferences with architects were generally held at this time, and no doubt at such sessions plans for the Taj Mahal were discussed. At six o'clock another round of business took place, now in a more informal atmosphere, with candlelight and whirling dancers. Again prayers were said, a review of the day's transactions was held, a light supper was served, and the emperor retired for the night. By ten o'clock he was usually in bed, listening to histories and romances — his favorites were the stories of Timur and Baber — and by ten-thirty he was asleep.

When the emperor was not in residence at the palace or in the field visiting outlying provinces, he was occupied with war. There, as in Agra and Delhi, he located himself at the center of all action. Military campaigns sometimes lasted many years, and the Moguls went to all possible lengths to make their military headquarters a portable model of the permanent court. Thus, most of these encampments were magnificent sights, carefully planned metropolises with two-story towers, multitudes of tents and shelters, bazaars, libraries, ateliers, farms, hunting grounds, and, as always, thousands upon thousands of people. Such encampments swarmed with camels and elephants hauling loads of ammunition, piles of hemp and hay, and plunder. Servants scurried in all directions, transporting art objects to the emperor's quarters for inspection or carrying messages and gossip from tent to tent. On the periphery of the camp, herds of sheep and fields of corn and rice were kept by a veritable army of farmers, and nearby lower-caste soldiers camped in cow-dung huts. Closer to the center of this martial city, bazaars crisscrossed and intertwined in imitation of the typical Indian marketplace. Glasscutters, prostitutes, tentmakers, goldsmiths, holy men — anyone who might be seen at the capital itself was seen here as well.

At the center of the cantonment, protected by walls and mounted guards, were the quarters of the emperor. Around his compound were tents: tents for salted fish and dried fruit, tents for saltpeter, tents for the emperor's betel and hashish, and a portable tent to which the monarch, obliged by Moslem law to pray five times a day regardless of external conditions, could withdraw in the midst of battle. Around this felt network were stationed the nobles with their wives and children as well as the officials of the court, the commanders and their officers — each living in a mobile house of a sumptuousness commensurate with his rank. If on the field of war a decisive battle was won or lost, this entire encampment was expected to be ready, within a day's notice, to advance or retreat to the next locale.

Between the world of battle and the world of pleasure, Shah Jahan still found time to acquaint himself with the subtleties of his government. Many documents from his day still exist, providing us with knowledge of each year of his long reign. Yet of his personal life relatively little is recorded, and we scarcely know him at all in the way we know several of his predecessors. He never wrote his autobiography, as had Baber and Jahangir, nor did he have a magnificent Boswell as Akbar had in Abu-l Fazl. Shah Jahan's biographers, beyond the immediate compliments with which they larded his name, were reluctant to discuss the psychology of their patron; and aside from flattering him with the usual bombastic titles — names like "Possessor of Power Over Planets" and "Index of the Book of Life"— they give us scarcely any intimate facts about his character. For this we must turn to the writings of Western travelers who came to Shah Jahan's India.

These European *voyageurs* scarcely represent the apotheosis of objective reporting — far from it. Writing for a commercial market in Europe, basing all their

To accommodate the expanding foreign market, seventeenth-century Indian craftsmen combined new themes with traditional handiwork. The intricately painted cotton bedspread below, made for export, depicts a party of Europeans (lower band) paying court to elaborately costumed Indian officials (upper band). A row of gifts divides the two halves; small figures fill most of the panels on the inner of two borders.

stories on hearsay and rumor (unlike William Hawkins or Sir Thomas Roe with Jahangir, no Europeans had first-hand knowledge of Shah Jahan's private affairs), these seventeenth-century travelers were less interested in producing authentic histories than they were in spinning good yarns. Moreover, even if they had wished to be totally accurate, the strange customs of the Indians — strange, that is, by Western standards — could only have confused writers who were inescapably bound by the prejudices of their own heritage.

It is also unreasonable to expect that European-born reporters would understand the mentality of a Mogul ruler, especially one such as Shah Jahan who claimed ecclesiastical as well as secular omnipotence. Unlike the traditional monarchy of the West — where the king was, at least in theory, subordinate to the power of church or pope — a Mogul emperor was himself the link between God and man. The emperor was a priest. He was the Jagat-Guru, the "Religious Leader of the World," and was accepted as such by a people who believed that the hand of God, working through fate, had placed him in this position. Thus a proverb at court declared: "If the King saith on noonday 'It is night,' you are to say 'Behold, the moon and the stars.'" Indeed, Shah Jahan claimed such power over the moon and stars: he actually changed the Mogul manner of measuring the hours and altered their calendar from solar to lunar time.

Bearing these facts in mind, we may put our European travelers on the witness stand and hear their entertaining testimonies. The first is the Frenchman, François Bernier, a friend of Louis XIV's finance minister, Jean Baptiste Colbert. Bernier disliked Shah

83

Jahan, who he tells us tried to subdue the arrogance of a certain Persian ambassador. The ambassador, it seems, refused to bow before the monarch. To humble the foreign upstart, the emperor erected a low wicket at the door of the throne room, thus forcing the Persian to enter doubled over. To Shah Jahan's surprise, when the ambassador arrived, he came through the low doorway backwards, presenting his posterior to the enthroned sovereign. The emperor was furious. "Ah, wretch, dids't thou imagine thou was't entering a stable of asses like thyself?" he roared. "I did imagine it," answered the ambassador. "Who on going through such a door can believe he is visiting any but asses?" This same emissary was asked by the emperor his opinion of the relative strengths of the Mogul and Safawid Persian states. The ambassador politely compared the Mogul Empire to a full moon and the Persian to a quarter moon. Initially pleased and flattered, Shah Jahan later realized that a full moon can only decline while a quarter moon can only expand.

At one time Shah Jahan was carrying on simultaneous liaisons with the wives of two of his courtiers. Each visited him in the palace at a different hour of the day. In the morning, when the first wife arrived, a beggar at the gates called out, "Oh, breakfast of Shah Jahan, remember us." In the afternoon, when the second wife appeared, the same beggar would shout, "Oh, luncheon of Shah Jahan, succor us." Such stories concerning the king's insatiable sexual appetite are common. Bernier and the Italian Niccolao Manucci claim that Jahan and his daughter Jahanara were involved in an incestuous relationship. Bernier also tells us that the emperor once caught Jahanara hiding a man in her chambers. To teach her a lesson, he ordered boiling water poured in the nook where the swain had sought concealment and where, to his great credit, he boiled to death without uttering a sound. These and other stories were as common then as are today's wild tales concerning nearly every figure who has the dubious fortune to become famous — all must be taken with a grain of salt. After the death of Mumtaz Mahal, the Great Mogul may have overindulged in the manner of his ancestors; it is indeed quite possible. But many of the enormities that Shah Jahan's detractors accuse him of have the obvious ring of outright calumny.

Concerning the Great Mogul's attitude toward his people, there are conflicting opinions. That it was a time of extreme hardship in many parts of India there is no question. In Gujarat, on the southwest coast of Hindustan, one of the worst famines of all time was raging. A description of this tragedy by an anonymous scribe is well known in Indian literature and is one of the most haunting passages ever written:

> Life was offered for a loaf and none would buy; rank was sold for a cake, but none cared for it. . . . for a long time dog's flesh was sold for goat's flesh and the powdered bones of the dead were mixed with flour and sold. . . . destitution at last reached such a pitch that men began to devour each other and the flesh of a son was preferred to his love.

Another report, equally grisly, informs us that:

> Men lying in the streets, not yet dead, were cut up by others and fed to living men, so that even on the streets and still more on road journeys, men ran great danger of being murdered and eaten.

How Shah Jahan reacted to this calamity is a matter of

some conjecture, although it is certain that he established soup kitchens, abolished all taxes in the area, and then proceeded to distribute some fifty thousand rupees to the starving Gujaratis.

Jean Baptiste Tavernier, another reporter from Europe, tells us that Shah Jahan "excelled other monarchs in good administration and in the order and arrangements of finances as well as the system of justice which was stern." This system of justice was indeed stern. According to Manucci, any official guilty of fraud was brought before the emperor, who it seems kept several baskets of poisonous snakes on hand for just such an event. The snakes were made to bite the delinquent, and he was left writhing in the emperor's presence until he expired. This method of punishment, though extreme, produced the desired results: graft was kept at a minimum, crime was greatly reduced, and the roads were so safe that a rich merchant could ride on any of them at night and not fear for his purse.

Tavernier also found Shah Jahan to be the most benevolent of despots. "This great king," he wrote, "ruled above forty years, not so much as a king over his subjects but rather as a father over his family and children." Tavernier tells of the emperor's great generosity, especially at the ceremony of Tula Dan. On these occasions, on a large scale supported by thirty-eight masts and standing forty feet high, Shah Jahan was weighed against gold coins, and these coins were immediately distributed to the poor. The Englishman Thomas Roe, on the other hand, had observed the Great Mogul as Prince Khurram and found him to be "so sordidly ambitious, that he would not have me acknowledge his father king, nor make any address,

nor deliver any presents, nor compliments of honor, but to himself." History, it seems, writes with mixed emotions about Shah Jahan.

If history is contradictory in its assessment of the Great Mogul, it is still a fact that he reigned over Hindustan for thirty prosperous and peaceful years. Despite the useless wars, the extravagances, and the squandered finances, he managed to keep his empire from collapsing beneath the weight of its own elephantine dimensions and ruled in a time that has often been called the golden age of Mogul India.

Toward the end of this rule, having grown somewhat bored with his administrative duties and having completed the Taj Mahal to his satisfaction, it entered the emperor's mind to construct his own mausoleum, a twin to the Taj Mahal. It was to sit across the Jumna River from the original, it was to be entirely black, and finally it was to be connected to the white Taj by a bridge of solid silver. Construction on this project, which surely would have been an excessive drain on the already overburdened treasury, reputedly began sometime in the 1650's, although no traces of its foundation have ever been discovered. Then in 1657 Shah Jahan was afflicted with strangury, spasmodic contractions of the bladder, and became so seriously ill that it appeared the sixty-five-year-old monarch was about to die. Three of his sons, Murad, Dara Shukoh, and Shah Shuja, hastily descended on Agra, ostensibly to pay last respects to their father but in truth to do battle for his throne. The fourth son, Aurangzeb, then a governor in the Deccan, held back.

To almost everybody's displeasure, Shah Jahan did not die. By the time he recovered, however, the desire

of his sons to enforce their father's retirement had become irrepressible, and each of them rose in rebellion. Aurangzeb now made his move. He first formed an alliance with Murad and together they marched on the forces of Dara Shukoh and annihilated them. Aurangzeb then proceeded to betray and execute Murad, chase a second brother, Shah Shuja, into a pirate-infested sea, and capture and decapitate Dara Shukoh, sending the head to his father, Shah Jahan. Nor was he finished. He incarcerated his own son, poisoned one nephew and imprisoned another, executed two of his grandnephews, and imprisoned his father in the Red Fort at Agra. In 1658, when all of these chores had been completed, Aurangzeb crowned himself the new Mogul emperor. His first act was to behead five hundred criminals as a lesson to all ruthless men.

For eight years Shah Jahan was confined to his rooms in the Red Fort, where he was consoled by Jahanara. Every day he sat at a window that looked out on the Taj Mahal across a bend of the Jumna River. His captivity was not what one would term uncomfortable, however, as his entire harem, all his wives, his eunuchs, dancing girls, singers, and servants were with him, as were his beloved jewels. In the beginning Aurangzeb begrudged his father these famous gems and sent his treasurer, Falud Khan, to make a report on their value. Falud Khan, after six months' study, replied that it would take fourteen years to go through all of them. Nor would the ex-emperor be duped. If they came to steal his pearls, he threatened to grind all of them to dust before anyone could find them. After several years had passed, Aurangzeb finally grew remorseful for all he had done and begged for his father's blessings.

Blessings were forthcoming, for Shah Jahan had grown devout in his last days and passed his hours absorbed in the Koran. Nonetheless, the story is told that he remained heir to the flesh until the end. One day, while adjusting his moustache, he saw in the mirror his two maid servants, Aftab, "the Sun," and Mahtab, "the Moon," laughing at his attempts to look youthful. To show them the virile stuff of which he was still composed, the old man swallowed a sizable portion of aphrodisiacs — and it killed him. At the age of seventy-four, the Great Mogul was dead.

Shah Jahan's body was placed on a simple cot in the Jasmine Tower. Next to his bed a tiny mirror was embedded into the wall, set at a certain angle so as to perfectly reflect the Taj Mahal. There he had lain while he was expiring, gazing at the reflection of his beloved wife's tomb, white and noble, across the river. And there the guards found him in the afternoon, his head still turned toward the mirror, his eyes still open and staring uncomprehendingly at the lovely image in the reflecting glass.

Deposed in 1658 by his ruthless and ambitious son Aurangzeb, the aged Shah Jahan (left) lingered for eight years as a prisoner in the Red Fort at Agra (below) — from which he was able to glimpse his beloved Taj Mahal in the distance.

V

A Visit to the Taj

Ali, the son-in-law of Mohammed, had said, "Shall I not give you orders that the Prophet gave me, namely to destroy all pictures and images and not to leave a single lofty tomb without lowering it within a span of the ground?" To hear was to obey. The Moslem warriors who came to India in the twelfth century, proclaiming their faith with blood-stained scimitars and boundless zeal, obeyed Ali's counsel to the letter; they spared scarcely a handful of the Hindu temples whose beehive-shaped towers once graced the Indian landscape. "It was the custom," reported Nizami, a Moslem writer, "after the conquest of every fort and stronghold to grind its foundations and pillars to powder under the feet of fierce and gigantic elephants."

From the beginning, Hinduism and Islam were irreconcilable. The introspective Hindu mind worshiped a multitude of gods in esoteric, mazelike sanctuaries, in temples dark and indeterminate. The mosques of the monotheistic invaders were open and simple. The peaceful Hindu sought no converts, searched no foreign lands in which to preach a creed. The Moslem lived to spread the faith with his sword — and even welcomed death in the service of the Prophet.

Yet the Moslem invaders insisted on carrying the interdictions of Ali one step further; they considered it implicit in his command that, after toppling the infidels' temples, they must raise their own. Soon on every hilltop, beside every road and marketplace, Moslem shrines appeared, and with them came something more unique, something rarely seen since the Buddhists had ceased to flourish in India some centuries before — the tomb. From the earliest days Hindus had practiced cremation, but the new masters of North India heeded the words of the Prophet and interred their dead in stone sarcophagi.

The first to construct such a tomb may have been the first of those peculiar Turkish rulers of India known as slave-kings. His name was Qutb ud-din Aibak and indeed he had been a slave — though a high-ranking one — under the command of an early Moslem invader, Sultan Mohammed of Ghur. His first act as king was to build a mosque just outside Delhi and near it he erected the Qutb Minar, a 240-foot tower, half victory turret, half minaret. Fashioned of red sandstone, with each of its five successively setback sections embossed with lacy relief, the tower was raised to proclaim the coming of Islam to India and was called the Axis of the Earth. It still stands, casting its elegant shadow across the stump of Aibak's nearby mosque, which has long since been laid to waste.

In 1205 Qutb ud-din Aibak also built the first Moslem tomb in India, the Arhai-din-ka-Jhompra, and his successor, Iltutmish, embellished it while building an even grander one over the remains of his young son. For more than three centuries, from 1206 to 1526, five dynasties of Afghans and Turks ruled Delhi. All of them fashioned tombs for their own remains and those of their closest kin. To the typical Islamic methods of construction the Afghans and Turks added their own imprint, a mixture of Hindu and Seljuk Turk styles. The result was far from elegant: massive twelve-foot-thick walls, low heavy domes, stone courtyards, and windowless façades. It was nonetheless a distinctive style and, in certain ways, a positive influence on the builders of the Taj.

With the arrival of the Moguls in North India, Indo-

Moslem architecture gave way to the structural styles of the conquerors. The first of these conquerors, Baber, was less an architect and builder than he was a gardener, more a soldier than either. The few leisure days he passed in India were occupied with the fabrication of watercourses and rose gardens rather than with the erection of tombs, and as a result no major structure standing today can definitely be attributed to his reign. The first mausoleum that can truly be called Mogul is the tomb of that luckless sovereign, Humayun. Likewise, it is Humayun's tomb that heralds the arrival of Persian ideals as an enduring influence in Indian architecture; indeed, the structure was designed by a Persian, Mirak Mirza Ghiyas. Located in Delhi, a few streets away from a modern hotel whose Palm Beach exterior contrasts peculiarly with the façade of its ancient neighbor, Humayun's tomb stands in the center of a rectangular walled garden surrounded by defunct parterres and a ragged line of date palms. It is worth close attention as an important precursor of the Taj Mahal itself.

On entering the gates of Humayun's tomb, one is immediately struck by the size of the building — vastness was a feature of much Mogul architecture — and by the surrounding park, one of the earliest attempts in India to unite garden and tomb. In the center of the compound stands the burial place, a two-storied structure set on a twenty-two-foot-high platform, bordered at the base by an arcade of doorways and topped with a double dome of white marble. Indications of the Persian influence are everywhere: in the floral mosaics, in the arched portals on each side of the tomb, in the inner octagonal burial chamber surrounded by apart-ments, and in the walled garden itself. Furthermore, all the above characteristics, plus the use of red and white stone for facing, the shape of the dome, the very blueprint of the building itself indicate that the builders of the Taj had visited this monument many times.

It also seems that they had studied and digested the best ideas from many other tombs in North India. The domed kiosks that grow like marble mushrooms across the top of Akbar's tomb at Sikandra are directly reminiscent of those that top the Taj. (Indeed the arrangement of subordinate cupolas around a central dome had been a feature of Afghan tombs for centuries.) The tomb of Shaikh Salim Chishti at Fatehpur Sikri, with its marble lattice windows and its use of white marble for the entire building, offers similar resemblances. And the *pietra dura* floral arabesques on the tomb of Itimad-ud-Dowlah in Agra seem like preparatory exercises for the jeweling of the Taj. The Hindu idiom can also be seen in the design of the Taj: in the shape of the cupolas and cornices, and in the central dome that springs from the design of a lotus inlaid at the top of the drum. In this building, too, one sees the Turkish, the Tatar, the Buddhist, even a hint of the Chinese. All are present, and for this reason art historians have battled ceaselessly over its "major influences," its "chief origins," and its "provenance."

Such arguments about the Taj Mahal miss the point. No doubt its builders borrowed what they considered the best of what was available, relying more heavily, perhaps, on the Persian simply because so many of the artisans were natives of that country. But they did more than borrow and rearrange. Their end product was indeed a synthesis, but so unique a synthesis that

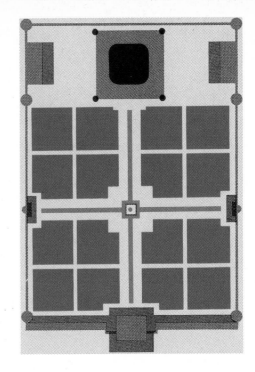

The gardens, walks, and subsidiary structures of the Taj Mahal complex are dominated and unified by the multidomed tomb (left), which shimmers in the waters of its reflecting pool. In the diagram at right, the main gateway is at bottom; the Taj, its minarets, and its flanking buildings are at top.

it emerges as an original work, something totally eclectic and yet imitative of nothing — in short, a completely new work of art.

Unfortunately this uniqueness is often lost to those who have never visited the Taj Mahal, lost because most are familiar only with the façade of the main building, photographs of which — along with such equally familiar works of art as Leonardo's *Mona Lisa* — have become the great visual clichés of our time. Despite its overexposure, this frontal view remains extraordinary; yet the Taj Mahal was meant to be seen from all angles, and the many surrounding structures — the gardens, mosques, minarets, walls, and tombs — were all designed to be part of the overall visual effect of the tomb complex.

A tour of the Taj Mahal starts with a bumpy ride along the main avenue leading out of Agra, a twisting, paved motor road that passes by a military installation, through a stretch of dusty farmland, and into a commons that was once an extension of the tomb grounds. (Today, dotted with litter and sleeping rickshaw drivers, the area is a municipal park.) Half a mile through the park looms the exterior gate of the compound. It is habitually surrounded by local villagers who vend sweets, lemonade, and alabaster models of the Taj in addition to offering the inevitable services: "Very good guide I will make you, isn't it, sahib?"

On either side of the road, just before one passes through the small outside gate, are two handsome octagonal buildings. The one on the left is called the Tomb of the Serving Ladies, but whether it ever served the function its title denotes is not known, for inside are two nondescript caskets, each without orna-

mentation and each without epitaph. Opposite is the Fatehpuri Mosque, a small, red sandstone shrine with a wide, arched doorway and space enough inside for a small congregation. Under British occupation, the mosque was taken over by lapidaries who turned it into a workshop and peddled mosaic platters on its steps. For that reason it is known as the Stone Cutters' Mosque. Eventually this activity was deemed a sacrilege and the mosque's religious function was restored.

Inside the gateway is a long arcade that was once the financial center of Mumtazabad. Faithful to its heritage, it is still lined with commercial endeavors — filmstands and curio shops, many of which are garnished with displays of the latest Hindu paperback books or billboards advertising hair oil. The end of the corridor opens into a central courtyard where cars are parked and visitors congregate before entering the main gate. Galleries of apartments that once housed the citizens of Mumtazabad enclose the courtyard. At either end is a tomb, one for Sati-un-nisa, favorite servant of the queen, the other for a royal wife.

In this courtyard stands the main gateway to the Taj and its gardens, a massive portal that opens to the south. Detached gateways were long a traditional feature of Moslem architecture and could be found fronting tombs and mosques throughout the East. They were, in effect, monolithic sentinels to keep people in or out — no minor function when so many jewels and so much gold was contained behind the walls. Furthermore, the gateways gave an atmosphere of importance to what lay hidden within, announcing by their grandiose presence that, since one was approaching a special place, one should assume a special attitude.

The arched entrance of the main gateway of the Taj Mahal (left) beckons the visitor invitingly. Crowning the three-storied structure are eleven kiosks atop matching open archways (above).

The grand main dome of the Taj Mahal, seen at left through a filter of greenery, is remarkably similar in form to the lowly haystack (right), common to the surrounding region.

Symbolically, to the Moslem, such an entranceway was the gate to paradise or the door to the womb of spiritual rebirth. Metaphysically, it represented the transition point between the outer world of the senses and the inner world of the spirit. A gateway was an overture in stone to the frozen music beyond.

"It is well to pause before entering," a guidebook to the Taj intelligently advises, "and admire the proportions and perfect taste of the decoration of this gateway; for afterwards one has no eyes for anything but the Taj itself." Standing one hundred feet high, the three-storied gate has a colossal archway at the threshold. A heavy door at the base is made from eight different metals and studded with knobs. Inside are countless rooms with hallways that wind and divide in such apparent abandon that they seem intentionally built to confuse; perhaps they were, for they have remained unused for three centuries and their purpose has long confounded the experts. On the southern façade, framing the central portals, are verses from the Koran, and here Shah Jahan's calligraphers have performed an ingenious optical trick: the size of the lettering that runs up and over the arch appears to be consistent from top to bottom. This illusion was created by gradually heightening the size of the letters as their distance from the eye increased; from the ground the dimensions *seem* the same at every point. This ingenious *trompe l'oeil* effect is used with equal success on the main doorway of the Taj itself.

From the gateway one gets his first look at the Taj, and for some this initial impression is forever surrounded by an almost occult mystique. Aficionados of varying persuasions will maintain that the Taj must first be seen by moonlight, or by the blue light of the dawn, or visited at noon when it is pearly white, or during twilight when the dome is pink and gold. They will also say that upon first beholding the Taj it will look small and far away, as if built in three-quarter scale. This is another optical trick. As one approaches, the illusion turns into another illusion: the building begins to grow, and continues to grow until, when the base is reached, it looms colossal. The dome especially seems to expand as one comes near, almost as if it were being slowly inflated.

This grand hemisphere, the finial of which stands two hundred twenty feet above the ground, is said to be derived partly from the round domes of the Turks and from Timur's tomb, the Guri Amir in Samarqand, partly from the work of architects in Bijapur who had already fashioned a Mogul-like cupola over the body of Mohammed Adil Shah, and who were, even at the moment the Taj was being built, topping the tomb of Gol Gombaz with a dome built to similar proportions. But not satisfied with such cut-and-dried explanations, Indian poets offer us more lyrical theories. The dome, they say, was inspired by the bell-shaped tents of the Tatars, by the summits of the Himalayas themselves, by clouds, by a ripe pear, by a human breast full of milk. Some have even suggested that the real inspiration was the bulbous haystacks that still abound in the fields outside of Agra and which do, indeed, bear a strong resemblance to the dome of the Taj.

From the entrance one also gets the first glimpse of the gardens, a green carpet running from the gateway to the foot of the Taj. In the mode of the Persian garden, this park is enclosed by a large wall, is divided

Persian influence is evident in the formal symmetry of the landscaped gardens of the Taj Mahal (right). At left is the ja-wab, *whose only purpose, seemingly, is to provide architectural balance for its mate, a functioning mosque on the opposite side of the central mausoleum.*

into squares, has a central fountain, and has a stone pavilion at each of its corners. In essence, it *is* a Persian garden, a form born and nursed to maturity in the desert flats of Persia, where men slaughtered one another over water rights and where an acre of shade in a treeless world of sand and sun was the goal of each day's journey. In fact, water and trees were so highly regarded by the desert dweller that in the Persian lexicon the words "garden" and "paradise" are the same.

Unlike other Oriental gardens — especially those of the Japanese, who learned to accentuate existing resources rather than formalize them — the Persian garden was artificially contrived, unabashedly man-made, based on geometrical arrangements of nature without any attempt at a "natural" look. The lines of trees and fountains, the neatly manicured flower beds in every quadrant, the marble canals crossing in mathematical regularity, all came closer to the formations of Versailles than those of Kyoto. But unlike the great formal European gardens, which were built for secular pleasures, the Persian garden was sacred ground, a tranquil oasis amidst the furor of temporal life.

Such gardens were introduced to India by Baber, who also brought with him the Persian infatuation with flowers and fruit, birds and leaves, things delicate, symmetrical, and organic. Baber, Akbar, Jahangir, all were men in love with nature. This passion can be seen in the art and literature of their courts, in their artists' paintings of forests and gardens, insects and antelope, and in the Mogul poets' incessant praise of the rose.

Like Persian gardeners, landscape architects at the Taj attempted to translate the perfection of heaven into terrestrial terms by following certain formulas. In Islam, four was the holiest of numbers — most arrangements at the Taj are based on that number or its multiple — and the gardens were thus laid out on a quadrate plan: two marble canals, each lined with trees — cypress trees symbolizing death, and fruit trees symbolizing life — crossed in the center of the garden, dividing it into four equal squares. These squares were in turn subdivided into sixteen flower beds, and in each were planted four hundred flowers. In the center of the four sections, halfway between the tomb and the gateway, stood a marble tank arranged to perfectly reflect the Taj in its waters. In it were placed goldfish, the descendants of which are said to swim there today. The garden contained many animals — peacocks, nightingales, rare fish. Guards in white robes patroled the grounds, chasing birds of prey and other predators from paradise; their weapons were peashooters. To the park came the Mogul nobility, there to spread carpets on the grass and picnic on sherbet and *kabab*. Sometimes a throne was brought to the grounds and placed in front of the fountain so that Shah Jahan could meditate on the bubbling waters and commune with the spirit of Mumtaz Mahal.

The emperor died and was also buried in the tomb, and his sons died, and the years passed. The waters dried up and the trees ceased to bear fruit. The looters and the grave robbers and the birds of prey arrived, and the garden became overgrown with weeds and vines. So it remained for two hundred years.

Today, happily, the gardens of the Taj Mahal have been partially restored. The cypress trees have been replanted, the lawns are kept clipped, and the vines

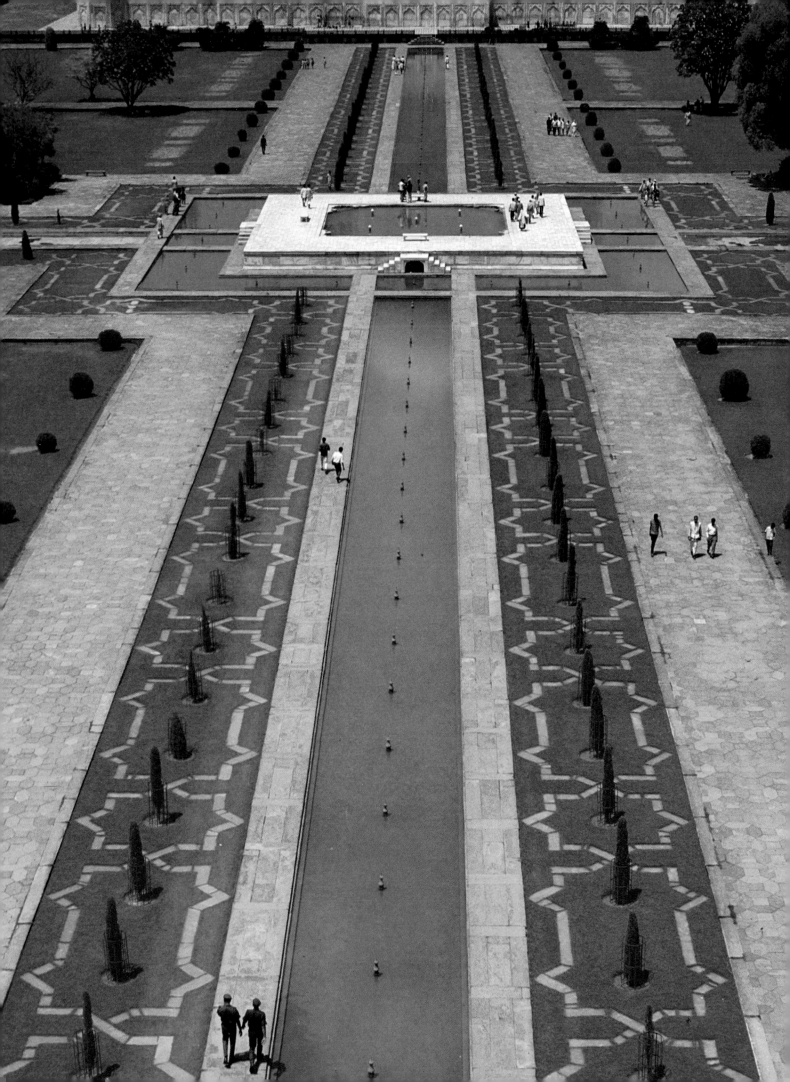

have been cut back, allowing a clear view of the building from any spot in the park. But the orchards, the gay parterres, the quaint beasts and fruit trees, all are gone; all, that is, except an old simal tree near the tomb that shows no signs of decay although it is said to have been in bloom before the Taj was built.

At the northern end of the garden is an enormous rectangular platform. In its center sits the Taj Mahal and on either side are buildings of red sandstone. The one to the west, a mosque, is three-domed, with the familiar *pietra dura* twining across its spandrels and, inside, a ceiling painted in a strange, hypnotic design. In all, it is a magnificent structure, and although it has the misfortune to sit next to the most majestic building in India, it is nevertheless architecture of genius. On the other side of the Taj stands the twin of the mosque, a parallel structure sometimes referred to as the *ja-wab*, or "answer." Because it faced away from Mecca it was never used for prayer and, as a matter of fact, its very presence there is something of an enigma. Was it a caravansary for pilgrims, or a meeting hall where the faithful gathered before prayer? More plausible is the theory that its purpose was purely architectural, to counterbalance the mosque and preserve the symmetry of the entire design on the platform.

Surrounding the Taj are its four famous marble minarets. Contrary to Aldous Huxley's assertion that they are the "ugliest structures ever erected by human hands," these towers are sometimes judged the most graceful in the world. Set on octagonal bases, they taper to a majestic height of 138 feet and are crowned with eight-windowed cupolas. Unfortunately, the view from these cupolas can no longer be enjoyed, for their spiral staircases are congested with colonies of bats. Each minaret is constructed off plumb, the one to the southwest by eight inches, the others by two. This was no accident, as it had been at Pisa. The builders of the Taj, always mindful of the mortality rate of buildings, designed the minarets to slant deliberately, so that if they ever tumbled they would fall outward, away from the all-precious Taj.

In the center of the minarets, standing like a "beautiful princess, surrounded by four ladies-in-waiting," is the Taj Mahal itself. Through its massive portal one enters quietly, with reverence. Inside is an enormous marble room. It is the octagonal burial chamber of Shah Jahan and Mumtaz Mahal. The chamber is dimly lit even at noon, for its only windows are perforated marble screens set far from outside illumination. In the center is the tomb of the queen and to one side is the casket of the emperor. Aurangzeb, who judged it a waste of funds to build separate tombs for any but his own wives, had his father placed there rather than in the proposed Black Taj — and there the marble coffin rests, an off-center afterthought, the only asymmetrical element in the entire design. But these caskets too might be called illusions, for the bodies of the emperor and his queen are actually interred in a small crypt directly beneath the great burial hall.

Nonetheless, the false tombs are far more noteworthy than their subterranean counterparts. Set with thirty-five kinds of rare stones, the mosaics decorating these cenotaphs are conceded to be the finest in existence, and equally fine is the calligraphy that sings the virtues of the emperor, his queen, and Allah — while it damns to hell the infidel. In the center of the

queen's sepulcher is the mosaic design of a slate, and
on the emperor's is the image of an inkwell, for it is
said that a king writes the desires of his soul on the
heart of a queen and that she must obey them in
heaven as she had on earth.

The almost polychromatic quality of the caskets
contrasts with the simple calligraphic designs on the
upper walls and complements the famous marble
screen that encircles the coffin. Octagonally shaped to
mirror the main gallery, the screen is carved in a filigree that can only be compared to lace.

The floral motif of the screen and caskets is picked
up on the lower walls of the main chamber, this time
in bas-relief, and it is repeated in the four octagonal
rooms that surround it. The latter were originally
meant to hold the remains of Shah Jahan's nearest kin,
but once more Aurangzeb failed to honor his predecessor's wishes, and they have remained empty to
this day. At one time musicians came to play sacred
melodies in these rooms, for the acoustics there are
wonderfully resonant. Still more resonant are those
beneath the main dome, a structure transformed by its
builders into a sensitive and subtle echo chamber.
Here the slightest noise reproduces itself in countless
celestial reverberations; it is impossible to say when
the sound stops and when silence begins. A dissonance
comes back the more dissonant, a harmony is amplified
beyond its original beauty. Whatever one sends out
comes back to him a hundredfold. After echoing for
many minutes, the sound rises in ever-decreasing cir-
cles to the dome, gradually blends into overtones, and
at last lingers only as distant, ineffable music over the
sarcophagi of Shah Jahan and his queen.

VI

Dynasty in Decline

The coming of Aurangzeb to the Mogul throne in 1658 heralded the decline of the dynasty. Traditionally cast as the heavy in the Mogul drama, Aurangzeb is still equated in India with cunning and suspicion, with intolerance, iconoclasm, and guile. Perhaps he has been judged harshly by history, perhaps not: Moslem historians pronounced him "the Man of Perfection"; Hindus still revile his name. It cannot be denied that he was a man of enormous energy and intelligence, a valiant soldier, a fair and patient judge, a competent administrator and a consummate statesman. It is also true that even before he was crowned he had murdered his brothers, incarcerated his father, and eliminated a small host of secondary kin. Of course, without the law of primogeniture to bridle the violence of inheritance proceedings, it had been traditional in Moslem countries for the sons of a deceased monarch to annihilate one another until the lone survivor could claim the crown. It was the law of *takht ya takhta* — "throne or coffin."

"In our quarter of the globe," wrote François Bernier, "the succession to the crown is settled in favor of the eldest son by wise and fixed laws; but in Hindustan the right of governing is usually disputed by all the sons of the deceased monarch, each of whom is reduced to the cruel alternative of sacrificing his brothers that he himself may reign, or of suffering his own life to be forfeited for the security and stability of the dominion of another."

More difficult to defend are Aurangzeb's endless wars, his persecution of the Hindus and other religious groups, his financial follies, and his treachery. Yet, strangely, it is less for these and other transgressions than for his so-called virtue that he so epitomizes the villain in Indian history.

Adhering to the rules of the Koran with the ardor of a fundamentalist, Aurangzeb considered it his duty to enforce these rules upon all his subjects. Once he had spoken, not all the tears of Hindustan could wash away his harsh decrees. A straw mat was his own bed, a simple white robe his garment. His fasts were frequent and so prolonged that friends feared he would starve himself to death. No meat passed his lips, no music reached his ears, no wine touched his palate — and so it was decreed for his subjects, who took to fields and cellars for their illicit entertainments. His orthodoxy allowed scarcely a moment away from the rigors of hard work and constant prayer, nor did it tolerate any breach of responsibility on the part of others. As the emperor pronounced moral homilies and dispensed alms with mechanical regularity, Moslem chroniclers at court styled him "the Living Saint" — before they, too, were banned. But such honorifics did not prevent his ministers and wives from trembling when he passed, and it was said that even the bravest of his five sons never received a message from his father without turning pale.

Throughout the empire, prescriptions for the pious life were spelled out to the letter. The cut of one's trousers must not exceed a particular length. Almonds and dates should be cultivated according to scriptural instructions. No one was allowed to drink from a silver cup or wear robes of gold. The signet of Islam was no longer imprinted on coins of the realm, lest the fingers of unbelievers pollute the name of the Prophet. Censors of public behavior eavesdropped on conversations, peeped into teahouses and into boudoirs, and reported the moral crimes of the nation in lengthy letters to Aurangzeb. Beards exceeding the length of four fingers were forbidden on the grounds that too much hair might impede the spoken name of Allah on its way to heaven; inspectors patrolled the avenues of Delhi, measuring suspicious-looking whiskers and administering shaves on the spot. "For the first time in history," writes the historian Stanley Lane-Poole, "the Mughals beheld a rigid Muslim in their emperor — a Muslim as sternly repressible of himself as of his people around him, a king who was prepared to stake his throne for the sake of his faith."

Aurangzeb ruled for over forty-nine years, the length of his tenure rivaled only by one other Mogul, his great-grandfather, Akbar. This long reign divided itself into two distinct and nearly equal periods. In the first, from 1658 to 1681, he resided in Delhi, a place that grew in importance as the city of the Taj languished into provincial obscurity. For the Mogul patrician, Delhi now represented all that was refined and fashionable in the empire; it was the Paris of its age, famous for its luxuriant parks and gardens, fine shops, broad streets, witty citizens, and opulent mansions where the most affluent of the realm congregated.

Even the emperor, by nature a recluse, bowed to the demands of contemporary elegance and appeared before the public in full regalia. Bernier, an observer of one such state affair, remarked:

The King appeared seated upon his throne at the end of the great hall in the most magnificent attire. His vest was of white and delicately flowered satin, with a silk and gold embroidery of the finest texture. The turban of gold cloth had an aigrette whose base was

compounded of diamonds of an extraordinary size and value, besides an oriental topaz which may be pronounced unparalleled, exhibiting a lustre like the sun. The throne was supported by six masay feet, said to be of solid gold, sprinkled over with rubies, emeralds, and diamonds . . . at the foot of the throne were assembled the *omrahs,* in splendid apparel, upon a platform surrounded by a silver railing and covered by a spacious canopy of brocade with deep fringes of gold. The pillars of the hall were hung with brocades of a gold ground, and flowered satin canopies were raised over the whole expanse of the extensive apartment, fastened with red silken cords from which suspended large tassels of silk and gold.

In the second period of Aurangzeb's reign, from 1682 to 1707, the emperor moved his court to the Deccan, the triangular portion of South India extending from Bombay on the west coast, across the subcontinent to the Bay of Bengal, and south to Mysore. There he remained until his death, not once returning north, even though his ministry there waxed lazy and corrupt.

The Deccan was all things to Aurangzeb. His father, then Prince Khurram, had been governor there when Aurangzeb was born, and in that place his mother, Mumtaz Mahal, had died during Shah Jahan's southern campaign. And there Aurangzeb dallied with the one great love of his life, the concubine Zainabadi. The two filled their days "with music and dance," and before Zainabadi's untimely death, Aurangzeb even consented to drink a cup of forbidden wine. "In after days," writes the Italian adventurer Manucci, "he was accustomed to say that God had been very gracious to him by putting an end to that dancing-girl's life, by

Despite Aurangzeb's hostility toward the arts, Mogul and Hindu craftsmen in regions such as the Deccan continued to produce works of outstanding quality: a mottled-jade sword handle in the form of a horse's head (below); an ivory chess set composed of Rajput warriors (right); and a painted and lacquered papier-mâché box (far right).

reason of whom he had committed so many iniquities, and had run the risk of never reigning through being occupied in vicious practices."

At the age of sixteen, Aurangzeb had received his first military command in the Deccan and had routed the forces of Jujhar Singh with such dispatch that Shah Jahan made him a viceroy. Then in 1645 he had been sent from the Deccan to neighboring Gujarat, and from Gujarat north to Transoxiana, with orders to wrest Samarqand from its mighty ruler, Abdul Aziz Khan. There, in the midst of a violent siege, Aurangzeb noted that the time for prayer was at hand. He dismounted from his elephant, knelt tranquilly facing toward Mecca, and began devotions while men died around him "like locusts and ants." "To fight with such a man is to ruin oneself," said Abdul Aziz Khan, and he withdrew. Aurangzeb had next been sent to capture the Afghan city of Qandahar from the Persians; but failing in that objective, he had returned to the Deccan in 1653 for a second term as viceroy. For the next five years he had waged war against the Deccani kingdoms, greatly increasing his martial skills. Finally, in 1658, having used the Deccan as a springboard, he usurped the Mogul throne from his father.

Aurangzeb, who came to his dictatorship under the name of Alamgir, "the World Seizer," was therefore a rugged soldier, one seasoned by the lance and well-schooled in fighting the infidel. His hatred for the enemies of the Prophet, however, was not strictly confined to Hindus. Moslems in the Deccan were of the Shiite branch of Islam; Aurangzeb, belonging to the rival sect, the Sunnis, shared his people's contempt for those Moslems who dared reject the first three caliphs as the

rightful successors of Mohammed. And although it was the Hindus who represented the idolatry he so despised, the Hindu Rajputs of north and central India had for many years been the strongest allies of the Moguls. Lane-Poole has written that to break faith with them would have been folly:

> These [Rajputs] were the bravest of the brave, born fighters, urged to fury by a keenly sensitive feeling of honor and pride of birth, and always ready to conquer or die for their chiefs and their privileges . . . [to see how] they rushed into battle maddened with *bhang* [hashish] and stained with orange tumeric . . . was a spectacle never to be forgotten. Had they all combined, the Mughals could not have stopped them; but happily they were weakened by internal jealousies and could be played off one against the other.

Since the days of Akbar, the Hindus had been treated as equals. They held public office, collected taxes, commanded armies, and shared in the prosperities and sorrows of the greater empire. True, the iron pillar of toleration forged by Akbar was at times reduced to a wobbly pivot by Shah Jahan, whose persecutions of the Hindus were not infrequent; but the builder of the Taj had grown mellow in his later years and peace had followed. Now a Moslem more intolerant by far than Shah Jahan held the royal standard, and the Hindus watched with trepidation as he abolished the practice of weighing himself against gold on his birthday, of anointing his Rajput generals' brows with sandalwood paste, and of showing himself at the Royal Window each morning. To Aurangzeb, such things smacked of idolatry.

For twenty years a nervous peace was maintained between the two communities while Aurangzeb focused all his hostility on foreign enemies, waging war on the northwest frontier and in Assam. Less rigid than in his later years, the emperor allowed the Hindus to go about their customs relatively unbothered and even recruited them for the royal ateliers, where some of the finest of all Mogul paintings were produced. Many artisans from Shah Jahan's era were still practicing at this time and consequently a certain greatness was also achieved in architecture. The tiny Pearl Mosque in the Red Fort at Delhi, perfect in its miniature dimensions and its three ivory-white domes, was the product of this period, as was the Badshahi Mosque in Lahore, a work of elegant proportions and arresting size. Less successful was the tomb of Aurangzeb's wife, Rabia-ud-Daurani, built at Aurangabad in blatant imitation of the Taj Mahal. The building lacks the graceful proportions of the Taj; the four minarets that surround it are almost caricatures of their predecessors in Agra. Indeed, this building is invariably cited as the prime example of the wane of Mogul architecture.

At the end of the twenty-year Moslem-Hindu détente, Aurangzeb could no longer repress his impulse toward proselytism, nor could he tolerate reports that the Hindus' "wicked science" was being taught to pious Moslems across his realm. In 1678, at the death of his most formidable Rajput ally, Jaswant Singh, the emperor sent troops to annex the maharaja's kingdom and forcibly convert his sons to Islam: with this one tactical blunder, Akbar's efforts to achieve reconciliatin between the two factions were forever erased.

Across India Hindus raised indignant cries. To silence them Aurangzeb — who had already razed their temples and schools in Benares — banned all Hindus from holding public office, from bearing arms, owning elephants, or riding in palanquins. During the first phase of this campaign he destroyed a Hindu shrine in the holy city of Mathura and placed its stone gods and goddesses beneath the steps of a mosque that he ordered built on top of the ruins; good Moslems could now trample idols on their way to prayer. Then, to rub salt in the wound, the emperor destroyed another cluster of temples in this same town and before leaving changed the city's name to Islamabad — "City of Islam." But worse than the deprivation and desecrations (in a single year 240 Hindu temples were demolished in one central Indian territory alone) was the reinstatement of the *jizya* tax, the rescinding of which was Akbar's greatest conciliatory gesture toward the Hindus. No law was more hated than the *jizya*, a poll tax on non-Moslems which demanded 5 per cent of each man's income for no other reason than his refusal to convert to Islam. Struck first in their churches and then in their pocketbooks, thousands of Hindus gathered at the Red Fort to protest the tax; when they refused to disperse, the emperor turned a pack of wild elephants loose upon them. This was the final outrage; throughout the empire men rose in revolt.

The Jats, once peaceful Hindu farmers, became marauders, and defeat after defeat could not quench their thirst for battle. The warrior clans of Rajputana, infuriated by Aurangzeb's treatment of Jaswant Singh's children, declared war. Despite feeble attempts at reconciliation, the Rajputs had taken their stand, and few would ride for a Mogul cause again. In the Punjab, the leader of the placid Sikhs, Guru Tegh Bahadur, was treacherously murdered at Aurangzeb's order; as a re-

sult, their new leader, Guru Govind Singh, vowed: "I shall make men of all four castes into lions and destroy the Moguls." In the north, the killing of a Satnami peasant by a Mogul soldier roused this militant sect of Hindu farmers to revolt, and thousands of them marched on Delhi, destroying mosques and picking up sympathizers along the way. At first the emperor's army was intimidated; rumors that the Satnamis were invulnerable and rode into battle on magic hobbyhorses were rampant. But Aurangzeb had magic, too — talismans, Arabic prayers on his banners, and, less arcane but equally effective, the imperial army, which he ordered to advance on the oncoming rabble. By nightfall, thousands of hapless peasants were exterminated, their slaughter serving only to further inflame the Hindus.

Most powerful of all the insurrectionists were the Marathas of the Deccan, whose descendants today populate the modern state of Maharashtra. They had tilled the land for many centuries, philosophically bending before every plunderer's blade. But in the third quarter of the seventeenth century, for no explicable reason, the Marathas' docility fell away and in its place appeared a martial energy of a kind rarely matched in India's past. This transformation was certainly due in part to the emergence of a Maratha hero, Sivaji.

Born in 1627 at Shivnar, the son of a well-to-do tax collector, Sivaji was brought up on stories of Hindu champions and martyrs by his mother, a pious Maratha lady whose influence did much to arouse patriotic and religious feelings in her son. As an adolescent, he sought out the company of local hill bandits and from them learned guerrilla warfare. By the time he was nineteen, he had pledged to free the Marathas from foreign

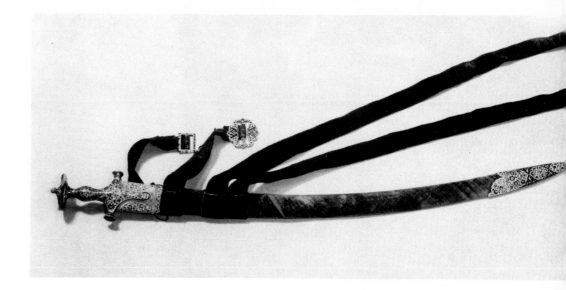

control; that same year, rallying a band of brigands, he began plundering caravans and local villages. Soon he had whole battalions of renegades at his disposal, and with them he began to expand his territorial holdings in earnest — during which time, in a manner atypical of his day, he outlawed the defilement of captive women and forbade all unnecessary carnage.

From 1647 to 1659, by bribery, sedition, cunning, and sheer charisma, the Maratha leader took dozens of hill forts in the Deccan, until his territorial holdings amounted to hundreds of square miles. Alarmed at Sivaji's advances, the governor of Bijapur mobilized his army and joined General Afzal Khan, who departed with a vow to bring the young pirate back in chains. This proved more difficult than anyone had imagined, however, and for some time Afzal Khan battled the Marathas to a standstill. Then one day a message arrived at his camp: Sivaji was willing to meet with the general and enter into negotiations.

When the day of the parley arrived, the two leaders, their armies camped on opposite sides of a plateau, walked to the appointed meeting spot in the center of the plain. As Sivaji approached, he bowed incessantly, smiled and fawned, dragged his feet, and even crawled, all the while vociferously complimenting the general and begging his forgiveness. In turn, Afzal Khan opened his arms to embrace the approaching prodigal. But when they met, the embrace quickly turned into a wrestling match and the wrestling match into a life-and-death struggle. Using steel "tiger-claws," which he had secretly affixed to his fingers, Sivaji tore into his opponent. When the grappling was finished Afzal Khan lay dead on the sand, and shortly thereafter Sivaji's

soldiers fell upon the hapless general's thoroughly confused troops and destroyed them.

Six years later the Marathas had become such a menace that Aurangzeb sent a large force to subdue them. After several bloody confrontations, Sivaji sued for peace, announcing that he himself would go to Agra and discuss the terms of a treaty — but only with the emperor. To Agra he did indeed go, to the palace of Aurangzeb; but when the court convened, the emperor made certain that Sivaji was placed with petty officers of the lowest rank in the back of the royal hall. This was too much humble pie for the headstrong Maratha to digest. In the middle of the stately proceedings, as sycophantic viceroys scraped and stooped before the Mogul ruler, Sivaji threw a tantrum. Screaming at the top of his lungs and stamping the ground, he ran at the emperor, shouted blasphemous remarks, and finally, in a fit of rage, collapsed insensate on the marble floor. Following this remarkable performance, he was carried to his rooms in the palace, where a heavy guard was posted at the door. There is little doubt that Aurangzeb would have disposed of him in characteristic fashion had not Sivaji made his famous escape in a large basket of fruit, which was carried out of the palace by a sympathetic peasant. Disguised as a fakir, he returned to the Deccan.

It was at this time that Sivaji began his most intense campaigns against the Moguls and against all other enemies of Maratha independence. In 1674, he crowned himself "King of Kings" — to the consternation of his adversaries — and he then proceeded to roll across the Deccan, harassing the imperial forces with ingenious guerrilla tactics and capturing every hill fortification

that lay in his path. Within ten years of his escape from Delhi, he had given the Marathas a working government and was master of a kingdom that ran like an archipelago across the Deccan. When he died in 1680, the foundations of Maratha power were so deeply based that only the strength of the entire British-Indian army would be able to subdue it 130 years later.

In his palace in Delhi, Aurangzeb was apprised of these and other ignominies and grew increasingly alarmed. Hindu and Shiite alike were dominating South India; they had to be stopped. The emperor proclaimed war on all enemies of the faith, and in 1682 he moved his armies and his court to the Deccan.

Twenty-five years later his war was at a stalemate and his empire was in chaos. Two Pyrrhic victories against Shiite kings, one in Bijapur and another in Golconda, had lost a fifth of the army, and another segment had succumbed to bubonic plague. Nor was Aurangzeb's heavy-footed infantry a match for the Maratha hill fighters, who raided the Mogul encampments continually for twenty years. These rugged warriors traveled as fast as deer, knew every rise and lane of the jagged Deccan landscape, could go days without water and weeks without food. When they fought, they gave no quarter; unlike the Mogul soldiers who, being mercenaries, fought only for pay, the Marathas battled for a cause that they considered holy.

Like Napoleon in Russia, Aurangzeb was swallowed up by the Deccan, the victim of an elusive, hydra-headed enemy, a merciless climate, and boundless tracts of empty space. In his many years of absence from Delhi, the dancing girls and wine venders he so despised had crept back to their stations. The treasury had been emptied by the endless wars, art and learning had atrophied and were only an echo of their former splendor, lawlessness was rife in towns and on the highways. Corrupt and careless without the emperor's supervision, the administration in Delhi had spawned a new breed of bureaucrats, less faithful to a cause than to the highest bidder. The Mogul Empire, vaster than ever before, was weak and rotten within.

In 1707, at the age of eighty-nine, his body racked with a hundred ailments and his prospects for a universal theocracy demolished, Aurangzeb died. Although his name was already well known in the West, where in 1675 it had inspired Dryden to write *Aurengzebe*, the emperor had few illusions about his own greatness. "I have not done well by the country or its people," he wrote shortly before his death. "My years have gone by profitless. Life is transient, and the lost moment never comes back. There is no hope for me in the future." From father to son, six successive generations of Mogul emperors had ruled India in the 181 years since Baber had seized power. In the succeeding 150 years there would be eleven more Mogul rulers, but the days of glory were definitely past.

Within a few decades of Aurangzeb's demise, the Mogul Empire collapsed at its center, the victim of foreign invaders and its own dead weight. Aurangzeb's religious policy had severed the right arm of the state, the Rajput imperium, and only a lax and indifferent army was there to replace it. Since the reign of Shah Jahan, when three failed attempts to capture Qandahar from the Persians had dispelled the myth of Mogul invincibility, the discipline and morale of the army had declined drastically. Although this army had grown gigantic, it was now filled with paid soldiers of dubious loyalties, drifters and freebooters recruited from within India and from places as far away as France. Moreover, petty jealousies among the officers mushroomed at times to such proportions that commanders failed to come to one another's defense unless it was established beforehand who would receive credit for the victory. This situation was exacerbated by "agreements" officers often entered into with the enemy; more than one battle was thrown in return for money or favors, and at times direct payment was a far more effective weapon for repelling an invader than actual martial force.

Moreover, the enormous expenses incurred by Shah Jahan and Aurangzeb so exhausted the Mogul treasury that as a last resort the government raised the taxes on farmers, who were already forfeiting a sizable portion of their produce to the state. The result of such exploitation was that the misery of the common people increased to unbearable proportions, starvation and famine invaded the most prosperous districts, and tax collectors and petty officials became more liable to bribes than ever before. This susceptibility to payoffs grew so widespread that the system of promotion by merit was practically nonexistent, and instead, government jobs were purchased outright by those who could afford the price.

The empire had grown too large and the stature of its rulers too small. Once a man like Baber had swum every river on his way into India; now a new breed of rulers rode to their engagements in gilt palanquins and silver howdahs — when they left their palaces at all. Hard work, tolerance, scope of vision, learning, all were replaced by indolence, disinterest, and ignorance.

The Mogul decline that followed Aurangzeb's death in 1707 was precipitated by a host of incompetent monarchs: Bahadur Shah (far left), who reigned for five years; Jahandar Shah (left), who was assassinated in 1712 after eleven months on the throne; Farrukhsiyar (right), first of four puppet emperors to rule in a single year, 1719; and Mohammed Shah (far right), noteworthy primarily for his longevity in office — twenty-nine dissipated years.

The Mogul aristocracy, jeweled and corpulent, grew soft in its love of leisure and became obsessed with its own political ends, while the empire dissolved. At court, intriguers gained the ear of men once faithful to the crown. Factions formed, self-interest prevailed. Bribery, blackmail, murder — all were the standard ingredients of the new statesmanship. Governors once allied with the emperor broke away to resume the petty disputes with their neighbors that had characterized all of India before Akbar. The Indian historian Sir J. N. Sarkar has summed up the period:

> There was no good education, no practical training of the sons of the Mughal nobility. They were too much petted by eunuchs and manservants and passed through a sheltered life from birth to manhood, every thorn being removed from their path by attendants. Early familiarized with vice, softened to their fibers by pleasure, they were yet taught to have an inordinately high opinion of their wealth and importance in the scale of creation.

By 1740, the Deccan was independent. The Punjab went to the Afghans, and shortly thereafter all of Afghanistan became a separate country. The Marathas, without the enlightened leadership of Sivaji, grew in lawlessness as they increased in strength and became "slayers of pregnant women and infants, of Brahmins and the poor, fierce in spirit, expert in robbing the property of everyone and in committing every sinful act." In 1737, the Marathas had moved north to take Malwa in central India. A few years later they conquered Orissa across the subcontinent on the Bay of Bengal, and they even led raiding parties to the fringes of Delhi itself. Their plunderings were complemented by those of the Jats who, in 1764, captured Agra and sacked the Red Fort, taking with them the Taj Mahal's finest gems and its silver gates. The Sikhs and a dozen lesser clans joined the movement for regional autonomy, and soon the empire simply disintegrated until all that remained was its once-great name.

At the time of Aurangzeb's death, however, Mogul ascendancy was as yet unchallenged. The first suzerain to inherit Aurangzeb's legacy was his oldest son, Muazzim, who, predictably, annihilated two of his brothers on the way to the throne. Once there he had coins minted in his name, as was the custom, and took the title of Bahadur Shah.

A generous old soldier of sixty-three, Bahadur Shah had spent part of his time languishing in one of his father's prison cells and all of it beneath his father's shadow. Yet despite his prior obscurity, he showed marked ability during his short term in office. His first task was to deal with the Sikhs of the Punjab, who were rapidly becoming a brotherhood of fanatical warriors. In 1710 their leader, Banda, had taken the town of Sirhind with uncalled-for brutality. "He butchered, bayonetted, strangled, hanged, shot down, hacked to pieces and burnt alive every Mohammedan in the place," writes a contemporary historian. "The mosques were polluted and burnt down and the Mullas, Maulavis and Hafizes were subjected to the greatest indignities and tortures." In retaliation, 60,000 soldiers from a number of Moslem territories were assembled and briefly allied in the famous battle of Gurdaspur, where the Sikhs were defeated and Banda was put to flight. Five years later this same Sikh leader is thought to have been captured by the Moguls and executed. But by then the Sikh com-

munity was thoroughly united. They continued to fight the Moguls "like lions" — eventually contributing to the dynasty's decline — and to this day the Sikhs remain one of the most cohesive and aggressive ethnic groups in all of India.

While dealing with the Sikhs, Bahadur Shah kept the Marathas at bay, reinstated the arts, restored a degree of toleration to official policy, and pursued a program of appeasement toward the Hindus that, though too little and too late, would nonetheless have caused Aurangzeb to gnash his teeth. Had this kindly, intelligent, and tolerant man lived longer, the decline of the state might have been delayed; but he died in 1712 and after the inevitable fraternal melee among his sons, Jahandar Shah emerged as emperor.

The eighth Mogul emperor ruled for eleven months, in which short time he turned the court into a brothel and the monarchy into a joke. Bewitched by a beautiful dancing girl, Lal Kumari, the new ruler surrendered all powers of state to his chief minister, Zulfiqar Khan, thus marking the emergence of the wazir as a primary force in the government. Then, at the bidding of his ambitious courtesan, Jahandar Shah promoted her relatives to high official posts, not neglecting the femme fatale's musician friends, nor old Zuhara, a vegetable seller from the bazaars. The finest mansions in Delhi were confiscated to house this group of misfits, all of whom were ennobled and given important-sounding titles. It was said by disgruntled members of the court that, "The owl dwelt in the eagle's nest, and the crow took the place of the nightingale." The emperor and his mistress passed their hours in idleness, tossing rocks at passersby from the roof of the Red Fort and

having boats sunk in the Jumna so that Lal Kumari could gratify her dream of watching women and children drown en masse.

While the couple caroused on the rooftops of Delhi, below in the dark marble halls of the palace the nobility was making its play for dominance. Prominent among the contenders were the Sayyid brothers, Husain Ali and Hasan Ali. Husain Ali had been governor of Bihar and his brother had once ruled at Allahabad. Both arrived in the capital city as men noted for their bravery and despotism, and both lived up to their reputations. As the emperor amused himself by having every tree in Delhi chopped down and by rolling naked with Lal Kumari in the streets of the town (both these incidents are well-documented), the Sayyids shouldered their way to power and finally into the emperor's very bedroom — where, at the feet of his beloved dancer, Jahandar Shah was strangled.

To the seat of power came Farrukhsiyar, first of the Sayyids' puppet emperors. Having spent two nights at the Taj Mahal in preparation for his coronation, Farrukhsiyar entered Delhi triumphantly in a macabre procession, the body of Zulfiqar Khan, Jahandar Shah's wazir, tied to the tail of his elephant. Trusting no one, intimidated even by children and servants, the new ruler quarreled with the Sayyids and was soon plotting wild schemes for their overthrow. His benefactors, who had hoped for a more tractable ward, eventually found these intrigues intolerable, and in 1719 they sent their assassins to his harem, the same apartment where Jahandar Shah had been murdered six years before. At first Farrukhsiyar hid from the henchmen in a closet, and when they found him he cowered behind the skirts of

his mother. But nothing availed. He was carried from the premises "bare-headed and bare-footed, subjected every moment to blows and the vilest abuse," and shortly thereafter was blinded, poisoned, and strangled. "Feeble, false, cowardly, contemptible," a scholar called the craven and short-lived emperor, adding, "It is impossible either to admire or regret him."

The next Sayyid candidate for greatness was a feeble consumptive who ruled for approximately sixteen weeks before expiring in a tubercular fit. He was replaced by another cipher, Shah Jahan II, who passed away in less time than his predecessor. Finally, the Sayyids, who by this time had justly been dubbed "the King Makers," raised to the throne a seventeen-year-old boy, Mohammed Shah, the fourth emperor to reign in a single year. But the new monarch proved to be less of a nonentity than those who had preceded him, and in a short time, with the help of nobles disenchanted by the Sayyids' machinations, he overthrew the King Makers and settled down to a relatively tranquil twenty-nine-year reign.

A handsome and cheerful youth, Mohammed Shah was equal to his ancestors in dissipation but he scarcely matched them in talent: he reigned but did not rule. A grandson of Bahadur Shah, he had spent his formative years as a pampered prisoner in the harem, and there he became addicted to the sexual and narcotic excesses that occupied the major part of his career. His sole interest seems to have been in animal combats, which he staged with the imagination of an impresario. (One such spectacle featured three bears, a goat, a ram, and a wild boar, all wrapped in tiger skins and trained to attack an elephant.) Nor did the young emperor re-

ceive substantial support from his chief ministers. The first quit in disgust after four years and was replaced by an aged inebriate named Qamar-ud-din Khan. On hearing that the Marathas had made themselves lords of Gujarat, Malwa, and Bundelkhand, that Bengal and Oudh were establishing their independence from the empire, that the nobles were dividing up royal territories among themselves, and that the emperor was comatose from all-night opium binges, the new prime minister assuaged his dejection by gazing philosophically at the trees and at the lotuses opening on the pond. "Emperor and wazir alike lived in total forgetfulness, of the business of administration, of collection of revenue, and the needs of the army," wrote a contemporary. "No chief, no man, thinks of guarding the realm and protecting the people, while disturbances daily grow greater."

During the early part of Mohammed Shah's reign the empire lived out its last splendid hours. Although the government was torn with dissension and rife with factionalism, life in Delhi was, on the surface, never more prosperous and brilliant. Painters and literati, ostracized by Aurangzeb, returned in force to breathe spirit into a defunct artistic tradition. They were accompanied by crowds of young fortune hunters, come to savor the tastes and titillations of cosmopolitan Delhi. Persian, Afghan, Sikh, Hindu, all intermingled in the bazaars with relative harmony for a few years. Gambling, dancing, and drinking reemerged and were joyously sanctioned by the smiling emperor, who waved majestically at the merrymakers from the Royal Window and sat enthroned in a Hall of Public Audience that dazzled newcomers. The treasury was empty and

the emperor was politically impotent, but commerce flourished, the army was enormous, and the streets of Delhi were gay. The Moguls were still, in the broadest sense, lords of India.

All of this ended abruptly in 1739. Three years previously, in Persia, an Afghan bandit-king named Nadir Shah had toppled the last of the Safawid emperors and, upon assuming leadership, had sent diplomatic envoys to Delhi. Through inefficiency rather than malice, the emissaries were detained in the Mogul capital, and the emperor failed to acknowledge further Persian communiqués. These and other insults provoked the new Persian rulers, and in May of 1738 Nadir Shah invaded the northwest frontier of India. Within a month he had taken Kabul; Lahore fell to him the following January. Sweeping through the Punjab, he was finally met by the Mogul army on the fields of Karnal, north of Delhi. Although the Moguls had superiority of numbers, they lacked the leadership and esprit de corps of their adversaries. Divided into splinter groups, pounded mercilessly with swivel guns, maddened by the charges of giant camels laden with explosives, the sons of Timur the Lame were no match for the Persians; before retreat could be sounded, 20,000 Indians lay dead on the Karnal plain — but a few miles from the fields of Panipat, where Baber's victory of two centuries earlier had marked the arrival of the Mogul dynasty.

Into Delhi rode Nadir Shah and behind him, bowing, saluting, trailed the vanquished Mohammed Shah. On his arrival, Nadir Shah made it clear to the emperor that his only demand was tribute money. He had no wish to remain in India, he said, and less to rule it. But while the two kings were coming to an agreement, out-

While local leaders proclaimed their independence from royal authority, the profligate Mohammed Shah (whose flaccid bulk is supported by litter bearers at left) continued to indulge in the pleasures of the court. Among those diversions was the popular pastime of opium eating (right).

side on the streets the Hindu festival of Holi was in full swing, and in the commotion someone started the rumor that Nadir Shah was dead. In response, hysterical citizens armed themselves and marched through the center of the city, murdering hundreds of Persian soldiers and plundering their garrisons. The next day Nadir Shah, very much alive, rode silently through the streets of Delhi, gazing at the corpses of his men and surveying the hostile crowds. Even as he passed, a bystander pelted him with a stone and a sniper killed one of the ministers riding at his side.

With a single motion of his sword, Nadir Shah gave the signal: the massacre started at eight in the morning and did not abate until three in the afternoon. From the roof of a nearby mosque, with what feelings we can only guess, Nadir Shah watched the grisly proceedings. A witness to the holocaust has left us his impressions:

On the morning of Sunday, 11 March 1739, an order went forth from the Persian Emperor for the slaughter of the inhabitants. The result may be imagined. One moment would seem to have sufficed for universal destruction. The Chandi Chowk, the fruit market, the Dariba Bazar, and the buildings around the Masjid-i-Jama were set afire and reduced to ashes. The inhabitants, one and all, were slaughtered. Here and there some opposition was offered, but in most places people were butchered unresistingly. The Persians laid violent hands on everything and everybody; cloth, jewels, dishes of gold and silver, were all acceptable spoil.

Delhi was looted, burned, and dismantled stone by stone — "The streets were strewn with corpses like dead leaves; the city was reduced to ashes and looked like a burnt plain" — and the following day the pillage con-

tinued. When Nadir Shah refused to allow inhabitants of the city to collect the bodies that had accumulated in heaps, plague broke out; when he sealed the doors of the granaries, famine followed. For eight weeks the plundering continued, and at the end of that time 50,000 people were dead.

Finally, after numerous supplications by Mohammed Shah, a halt was called to the slaughter, and the Persian army marched out of Delhi — but not before loading itself with enough spoils to eliminate all taxes in Persia for the next three years. An eyewitness recorded the scene:

All the regal jewels and property and the contents of the treasury, were seized by the Persian conqueror in the citadel. He thus became possessed of treasure to the amount of sixty lakhs or rupees and several thousand Ashrafis; plates of gold to the value of one crore of rupees, and the jewels, many of which were unrivalled in beauty by any in the world, were valued at about fifty crores. The Peacock Throne alone, constructed at great pains in the reign of Shah Jahan, had cost one crore of rupees. Elephants, horses and precious stuffs, whatever pleased the conqueror's eye, more indeed than can be enumerated, became his spoil. In short, the accumulated wealth of three hundred forty-eight years changed masters in a moment.

Thirty-two years after the death of Aurangzeb the Mogul Empire was no more. With the conquerors went not only the treasury, but also the last of the empire, Afghanistan and much of the Indus valley. With it also went the prestige that had kept the Mogul name sacrosanct, and in later years, despite brief minor revivals, the empire existed in title alone. Delhi was a tiny island

The humiliation of the weakened Mogul Empire was capped in 1739 by the invasion of the Persian ruler Nadir Shah (opposite). After sacking Delhi and massacring its population, the conqueror departed with most of the Indian treasury — including Shah Jahan's Peacock Throne — as booty.

amidst a churning ocean of emerging political powers.

For nine more years a stunned and saddened Mohammed Shah remained on the throne, incapable of doing anything, master of a charred and desolate ghost city. When he died in 1748, he was followed by Ahmad Shah, a debauched nonentity who, for the six years of his reign, remained under the firm control of his eunuchs and wives. Although his wazir, Safdar Jang, sincerely attempted to bring order to what remained of the government, Safdar Jang's successor, Imad-ud-Mulk, had less allegiance to state or crown. "The emperor has shown his unfitness to rule," he and his followers declared. "Let him be deposed and a worthier son of the house of Timur raised to the throne."

This worthier son, Alamgir II, was a weak and pious aristocrat who was content to remain in the mosque while his treasury was stripped, his wives were starved, and his capital city was sacked by another Persian terror, Ahmad Shah Durrani, who reduced Delhi once again to chaos and rubble. When Alamgir II finally showed interest in his job, his wazir became annoyed and had the upstart thrown out a palace window. Eventually some faithful subjects retrieved the body of the poor emperor from the riverbanks and interred it within the walls of Humayun's tomb.

In 1759 Alamgir's son, Shah Alam II, was crowned emperor. During the forty-seven years of what can only with reservations be termed his reign, Shah Alam II was the prisoner of bandits, the puppet of the Marathas, the mouthpiece of various Bengali potentates, and finally the pensioner of the British, who marched into Delhi in 1803 and found the blind and tattered old king cowering beneath the royal canopy.

Masters of India but a few years later, the British allowed the charade of Mogul suzerainty to continue through the reign of Shah Alam II's successor, Akbar Shah II, whose court in Delhi was described by Bishop Heber in 1824 as "dirty, lonely, and wretched; the bath and fountain dry; the inlaid pavement hid with lumber and gardener's sweepings, and the walls stained with the dung of birds and bats." But in 1857, the year of the Sepoy Mutiny, when native sepoys rebelled against their British officers and burned Her Majesty's garrisons to the ground, this final concession to the Mogul heritage was ended. Whether by choice or force — it has never been established — the incumbent emperor, Bahadur Shah II, was implicated in the revolt; and when the mutineers were finally defeated and Bahadur Shah II was brought to trial, a drumhead court sent him into exile. Thus Bahadur Shah II, a surprisingly brilliant poet and a truly sensitive man, was carried off in a bullock cart to Rangoon. There, in a country far from the Taj Mahal and farther from the homeland of his ancestors above the Hindu Kush, the last of the Mogul emperors lived out his days.

VII

The British Raj

In narrating the final episodes in the story of the Taj Mahal it is necessary to review the history of the British in the East — how they got to India and what they did once they arrived. To do this we must return to India as it was before the European invasion.

The subcontinent had been a source of fascination to Western man ever since Alexander the Great marched through the Khyber Pass and fought the last of his major battles on the banks of the Hydaspes River. Monsoons, the horrors of rain forest warfare, the terrifying gray monsters called elephants that the enemy rode to battle — all demoralized the young conqueror's men to such a degree that his Macedonian officers mutinied. Given no alternatives, Alexander abandoned further thought of Indian conquest, and in 326 B.C. marched sadly out of Hindustan. As he departed, the curtains of the East closed tightly behind him and did not open for more than 1,800 years.

Then, at the end of the fifteenth century, proclaiming the impending age of colonialism, the route to the fabled Indies was opened by the epochal voyage of Vasco da Gama. Arriving at Calicut on the southwest coast of India in 1498, the Portuguese explorer erected a stone pillar to commemorate his arrival, loaded six Hindus aboard the royal frigates, and cruised back to Portugal. He displayed these curious souvenirs — along with the treasures he had amassed on his journey — to King Emanuel I. The king liked what he saw and financed additional trips to the Indies. By 1510, thousands of Portuguese settlers had traveled to the East and, under the guidance of Affonso de Albuquerque, had made the city of Goa the capital of Portuguese India. With the new settlers came missionaries, and

with the missionaries came that most persuasive of religious instruments, the Inquisition; by cajolement, forced conversion, and torture, the Portuguese turned the native inhabitants into Christians and Goa into a theocracy. For seventy-five years these zealous foreigners ruled the major trade routes to India.

But the gates of the Orient had been unlocked, and at the end of the 1500's, on the eve of their century of artistic and political greatness, the Dutch came to the East. Their first expedition was headed by Cornelius de Houtman, who reached Java in 1596. There, in the village of Bantam, he constructed the first European trading post in the East Indies. This colony was an immediate financial success, and six years later the United East India Company of the Netherlands was born. Under its flags the Dutch became overlords of the East Indies and masters of the enormously profitable spice trade with Europe.

Impressed by the success of the Hollanders, a group of London businessmen met to discuss the formation of an enterprise similarly dedicated to Oriental trade. In 1600, under a charter granted by Queen Elizabeth I, the British East India Company was founded. Within a short time, representatives of the company were shipping out for Eastern shores. These Englishmen went not as soldiers, not as statesmen or reformers, but as merchants, simple British traders with a taste for adventure and a passion for speculation. They did not indulge in the type of territorial expansion that their countrymen were currently carrying out in the Americas; under the watchful eyes of Jahangir, they didn't dare. Indeed, the sense of allegiance the English in India felt toward the Moguls was matched only by their loyalty to the British crown, and for many years they followed a policy of scrupulous nonintervention in Indian political affairs. It was only later, as their position in India became consolidated and that of the Moguls tottered, that the English became more ambitious. This happened so slowly, with such subtle transitions, that conqueror and conquered alike scarcely noted the changes taking place until the patterns of usurpation were irrevocably drawn.

In the beginning, the East India Company's only concern was to corner the market in spices. Modern man with his chemical surrogates no longer relies on herbs and condiments, but for a seventeenth-century European scarcely a drop of wine or medicine, of perfume, dye, or foodstuffs could be prepared without them. Thus, to control the spice trade was to control the commerce of the world. Moreover, as trading between East and West increased, it appeared that India was a seemingly endless source for many kinds of trade goods — indigo, saltpeter, raw silk, cotton, sugar. It also appeared that Europe, already overpopulated and undersupplied in Malthusian proportions, would find it increasingly difficult to continue its extravagant lifestyle without exploiting foreign markets.

To meet these growing demands, British ships sailed to the East Indies in quest of pepper — only to find the Dutch entrenched with cannons and mercenary soldiers. After several unsuccessful trips to Java, they changed their course and headed for India — where the Portuguese, jealous of all interference, harassed the newcomers. But the British seafarers, men who had turned back the Spanish Armada, would not be bullied. In 1612 and again three years later, they met the Portu-guese on the Arabian Sea and destroyed them — much to the delight of Emperor Jahangir and the Mogul aristocracy of his courts.

Jahangir liked these Englishmen. They were swift on the ocean and mannerly in his courts, not at all like the hot-blooded Portuguese envoys who, with gesticulations and genuflections, promised allegiance even as their pirate ships sank Jahangir's vessels and their priests tortured his people. And were these English not of potential value to the Great Mogul? Their power on the ocean was indisputable, reasoned Jahangir; why not make them his naval auxiliaries and thereby control India's waters as well as her plains?

By the time the first English ambassador, Thomas Roe, arrived in India in 1615 the emperor, in return for protection on the high seas, had already given the East India Company permission to found an office in Surat, and that colony, some five hundred miles north of Goa, rapidly became the capital of British India. Roe was ambitious and charming; his diplomacy was flawless and his purpose clear. "Let this be your golden rule," he wrote to the officers of the company, "that if you will seek profit, seek it at sea and in quiet trade." By the time he left India in 1618, the quiet "factories" in Agra, Broach, Ahmadabad, and Surat were all established enterprises.

Not actually factories in the modern sense — they did not manufacture anything — these establishments were originally warehouses, clearing stations where goods purchased in the interior were stored until the arrival of cargo vessels from London. But as the years passed, they expanded. Brigands were a constant threat and walls were erected around the factories to protect their

Growing British involvement in Indian affairs during the eighteenth century had a marked influence on the arts. The startling spectacle at right — of an unmistakably Indian gentleman relaxing at the shore in a Queen Anne chair while smoking a water pipe — is the work of a native painter. The undisguised hostility engendered by the East India Company is revealed in an ingenious wooden effigy (left) of a tiger mauling a company employee. The bizarre toy, originally part of a local ruler's collection, was captured by the British in 1799 and sent home to England.

inhabitants; in this way the factories became forts, and the forts in turn became thriving commercial centers. Business was good and the East India Company kept enlarging its sphere. Traders, adventurers, bored teachers and bullied clerks, whole families migrated to India, and with them came soldiers, hired to protect the company's interests. By 1614 the company had a small fleet at its disposal, and within fifteen years twenty-three more outposts had been founded in its name. When the profit reports arrived, King James I was so pleased that he renewed the East India Company's charter "for ever."

"For ever" lasted ten years. James I's successor, Charles I, busy with the domestic intrigues that would soon cost him his head, failed to appreciate the value of foreign markets and refused to renew the company's charter. Trade in India was further neglected when the English Civil War broke out; and when Cromwell helped himself to the company's coffers, taking a "loan" of £46,000, the company prepared to close its offices. But at the last moment Charles II was raised to the throne, and with the Restoration in 1660 came new support for interests abroad.

In 1640, the British had built Fort Saint George in Madras, on India's east coast. In 1651, Shah Jahan had granted them trading rights farther north and they expanded into Bengal. Settlements were founded in Porto Novo, Cuddalore, Mysore, and all along the southern coast. In 1670, the island of Bombay, ceded to the British as part of the dowry of Charles II's Portuguese bride, replaced Surat as the capital of British India, and in this island city the semblance of British military power began to crystallize. Yet the notion of actually conquer-

ing the Indian subcontinent for Great Britain had so far occurred to only one man.

He was Sir Josiah Child, an outspoken officer of the East India Company who dominated its policy for more than twenty years and who once remarked that "the laws of England are a heap of nonsense, compiled by a few ignorant country gentlemen." In 1691, irked at the perennial conservatism of the East India Company, Child broke away and founded his own organization, the New England Company. Before the two associations merged a few years later, Sir Josiah made the statement that would endear him to Victorian posterity. It was time, he said, to lay "the foundations of a large, well-grounded, sure English domination of India for all times to come."

As profits rose on the boards of the English counting-houses, jealous eyes across the channel had focused on the figures. Soon the French decided that they, too, wished to share in the 22 per cent annual returns. In 1664, under the auspices of Louis XIV's financial minister, Jean Baptiste Colbert, the French founded their own version of the East India Company, the Compagnie des Indes Orientales, and sent boatloads of merchants off to India.

In the first half-century of colonization, the French founded factories in Surat, Chandernagor, Musulipatam, Calicut, and Pondicherry — this last, south of Madras, becoming the French capital. All the while the French were fortifying these towns and concluding agreements with local princes. Chief among the conciliators was the French governor, Joseph François Dupleix, a cunning judge of political winds and an Oriental monarch at heart. Dupleix built a local army

In retaliation for the capture of Calcutta in 1757 and the death of British hostages imprisoned in the "Black Hole of Calcutta," the East India Company empowered Robert Clive (left) to lead an army against the rebellious nawab of Bengal. Clive's resounding victory initiated a new era in British-Indian relations, one that was consummated in 1773 by the appointment of Warren Hastings (right) as first governor general of Bengal.

of Indian villagers, drilled them with European discipline, armed them with the latest Western weaponry, and thus founded the sepoys, native soldiers trained and commanded by European officers. With these highly efficient pocket armies as bait, the French governor lured several neighboring chieftains to his patronage. He sponsored them on their way to local thrones, made them dependent on him for protection and beholden to him for their crowns. Soon he established a nexus of regional partnerships throughout South India, all the members of which paid tribute to the French company and pledged themselves to the defense of its interests.

Dupleix continued to enlarge his realm, but in 1740 Frederick the Great seized the Austrian province of Silesia and plunged a half dozen European nations into the War of the Austrian Succession. As usual, France and England were enemies, in India as well as on the continent. Sensing disaster, Dupleix tried to keep the peace, but a fleet of British men-of-war arrived at Pondicherry and a series of fierce naval engagements ensued. In 1748, the Treaty of Aix-la-Chapelle brought a temporary halt to the hostilities, but three years later the armies of the English, led by an ambitious young soldier named Robert Clive, broke the power of the French. Trading rights in the Carnatic and Bengal were ceded to the British East India Company, and Dupleix was called home. Although his machinations later became the prototype on which many British governors based their politics, Dupleix's talent went unrecognized in France — he died in disgrace — and the French, after several more disastrous encounters with the British, thought the whole business not worth the price

in men and money and withdrew from Indian affairs.

While the French were evacuating India and the Mogul Empire was disintegrating, the British were growing bolder. Their soldiery, once a small band of native policemen, had gradually been enlarged, trained, armed, disciplined, and indoctrinated — until by the mid-nineteenth century its members had become the sepoy army. With this new muscle behind them, the British dotted the high walls of their cities with cannons, ostensibly in defense against the French but in fact to make themselves impregnable to French and Indian alike. These fortifications were often erected without the consent of local rulers to whom the British were, in theory, subject; and the rulers, quite rightly, took these fortifications to be a challenge to their authority. Finally and inevitably there was trouble.

In 1756, the British armed Fort William at Calcutta without obtaining official sanction from the nawab of Bengal, Siraj-ud-daula. Siraj, already fanatical in his fear of the brash Western merchants, could tolerate their ambitions no longer and sent his troops to capture the fort. Poorly defended, the British outpost fell within four days.

In the cellar of Fort William was a brig measuring eighteen feet by fourteen feet, a chamber no larger than an average-sized livingroom. Into this dungeon 145 Englishmen and one Englishwoman, all prisoners, were crammed by the nawab's officers, and by morning 123 of them — the precise number has often been argued — were dead from suffocation. A minor atrocity, perhaps, on the measuring stick of an Oriental despot, but the incident outraged British subjects, who dubbed the prison the "Black Hole of Calcutta" and cried out

for vengeance. When word of the incident reached the British offices in Madras, the East India Company overrode its policy of nonintervention and sent an avenging army under Robert Clive to punish the nawab. On June 23, 1757, the forces of Siraj-ud-daula met those of Clive on the fields of Plassey, near Calcutta, in the first important military engagement ever fought between the British army and the Indians.

In a book of great battles Plassey would scarcely merit mention in the footnotes, and only because of its historical significance rather than the brilliance of its rival tacticians. With a force of nine hundred Europeans and fifteen hundred Indians, Clive marched against the nawab's preposterously ill-equipped battalions. Most of the battle was decided by artillery fire, which happened to be strongest when coming from British guns, and by an idiotic charge made by one of Clive's majors that was so foolhardy it succeeded. At the end of the day, sixty-five British and five hundred Indians were dead, and Calcutta belonged to the company. Following the encounter, Clive installed a puppet nawab on the throne and left for England. The new puppet and the puppet after him would not jig to England's horn, however, and the Bengalis were disciplined once again in 1764, this time at Buxor, a larger and more intelligently fought battle than the previous one. Buxor finished what had been started at Plassey; the British now controlled not only the trade in Bengal but Bengal itself — and the implications were enormous. For the first time, the East India Company became a military as well as a commercial power, perhaps the match for any other in India; and for the first time, the British were landowners, lords over nine hundred miles of

Bengalese plains. In the home office, the perspectives were changing: why remain a merchant when one can become a king?

Robert Clive — now a great hero in England, described as "a heaven-born general" — returned to Bengal as governor and continued to rule with a new nawab as his mouthpiece. In due course Clive returned home, and he was succeeded by several mediocre diplomats. Then in 1772, Warren Hastings, who became the first governor general of Bengal, arrived with orders to "stand fast as *diwan* [ruler]" — which meant simply to dispose of the nawab and rule directly.

Warren Hastings had come to the East in 1750. Unlike many of his contemporaries, he loved India, learned several of its languages, and befriended many of its people. Twenty-two years of dealing with Hindustani plutocrats had endowed him with a consummate sensitivity to the Indian psyche, and he used this to its fullest advantage while still complying with the orders of his superiors. "We arm you with full powers," his superiors wrote Governor General Hastings from London, "to make a complete restoration."

Hastings's first concern was to centralize the company's authority and to transform it from a mercantile administration into a working political machine. To do this he reduced the nawab to a pensioned nonentity and then eliminated all indirect collection of revenues in Bengal, appointing Englishmen to call for payments directly. Commissions and salaries were fixed, internal corruption was curbed, land was surveyed and maps drawn, officially delineating British boundaries for the first time. Hastings introduced English law to India, set up a supreme court presided over by a British lord,

Thomas Daniell, a landscape painter
and engraver, was one of scores of
English artists who flocked to India in
the late eighteenth century. His
watercolor impressions of Calcutta
reflect the ambitious building schemes
of the foreign residents of the city. At
right is his view of the Old Court
House and the Writers' Building, a
home for young employees of the East
India Company — a prospect that must
have reminded homesick Londoners of
Regent Street. The solitary obelisk
opposite the Old Fort (above, left) is a
memorial to those who died in the
infamous "Black Hole" dungeon.

and in the first important instance of company justice being administered to a non-British subject, hanged a raja for forgery. Calcutta was officially made the capital city, the treasury was moved there, and colleges, residences, and administrative buildings were erected on its avenues. While making these adjustments in the inner workings of the company, Hastings also enlarged the sepoy army to such an extent that it successfully fought off the Marathas and the Rohilla Afghans, a tribe of mountain men established in the northern river valleys of India. In short, he laid the foundations of British power in India — and for this he was slandered and impeached.

Hastings's impeachment trial in 1788 was a cause célèbre that included the two most famous statesmen of the time, William Pitt and Edmund Burke. Hastings by then had many enemies in London. His methods abroad had not always been exemplary, although most returnees from India's political front knew the small niche that the god of ethics occupied in the pantheon of Indian diplomacy. He was brought before the House of Lords under twenty-one propositions of impeachment and was accused of "wanton and pernicious misuse of powers in overturning the ancient Establishments of the Country." The trial dragged on for seven years, and by the time Hastings was acquitted his name had been besmirched, his pockets emptied, and his chances of gaining further office destroyed. "I gave you all," the saddened ex-governor general said, "and you have rewarded me with confiscation, disgrace, and a life of impeachment."

The gap left by Hastings's departure from Bengal was indifferently filled by several governors general,

one of whom, Lord Cornwallis, had recently played his famous part in the American Revolution. In 1797, Richard Wellesley was appointed to the post, and for the first time a representative of the East India Company openly proclaimed his intent to establish British omnipotence.

By this time the Mogul Empire had completely fallen apart and its components were reintegrating themselves in clusters of independent territories across India. These Wellesley methodically commenced to carve up and digest, piece by piece, province by province. The ambitious governor general first bullied the nizam of Hyderabad into accepting British protection (and hence vassalage) and then bombarded the powerful tippu of Mysore into surrender, putting a British-controlled figurehead in his place. He proceeded to follow a program of aggression against the Marathas and subdued them with the help of his brother, Arthur, who later would achieve immortality as the Duke of Wellington. Within six years, the British owned the Carnatic, most of the Deccan, Oudh, Bengal, and Bihar — an area encompassing more than three-quarters of the Indian subcontinent.

Secretly gratified, the home offices in London were nevertheless a bit nonplussed by the swiftness of these acquisitions, and as a matter of "principle" Wellesley was recalled. He would die many years later, much honored but totally mad with delusions of grandeur and insanely jealous of his more famous brother.

Although lapsing at times into the policy of nonintervention, Wellesley's successors were in truth given no choice but to pursue his program of territorial aggrandizement. The Marathas were defeated for the last time,

invasions were launched into Nepal, the annexation of Rajputana and other remaining territories was effected, and by 1820 all but the Punjab looked to the East India Company for laws and protection. This final impediment to British power was eliminated when Lord Dalhousie conquered the Sikhs and annexed their land in 1848. By the beginning of the second half of the nineteenth century the British had succeeded in making themselves lords of all India.

The change, however, was not yet complete. In the process of appropriating India, the British understandably had not made themselves popular. There were many reasons for this; one of the principle ones was their insistence on reforming the natives as well as conquering them. The rites of suttee and idol worship, of ablution and prostration, all were distasteful to the sensibilities of the British. These they attempted to eradicate by armed force or through the absurdly alien methods of Western jurisprudence. The Hindu caste system was especially repellent to the invaders — although it must be said that their own was almost as advanced as the one they deprecated. They ignored its taboos, belittled the religious basis on which it was founded, and upon occasion, to the fury of the Hindus, tried to obliterate it completely. At the same time, the sepoy armies were now composed of ten Indians to every one Englishman. Many of these native soldiers were dissatisfied with their wages and unhappy at being shipped off to foreign fronts; some simply resented Westernization. As a result, the sepoys were restless and discipline was lax. These problems once caused Governor General Lord William Bentinck to remark that the army he maintained in India was unquestionably "the

Britain's seemingly secure control over the subcontinent was endangered in 1857 by a major uprising of Indian soldiers (far left). Ironically, the cannons used to quell the Sepoy Mutiny were drawn by native elephants (left).
Overleaf:
Relishing their role as the new rulers of India, the British revived many of the customs of their Mogul predecessors. Undeterred by the staid portraits of his ancestors, an English nabob succumbs to the temptations of hookah and harem.

most expensive and inefficient in the world."

In 1857 the situation finally came to a head. A new rifle, the Enfield, was supplied to the sepoy army. It fired a special cartridge that could be loaded only after the cap had been bitten off. Almost as soon as these guns arrived, a rumor was circulated that the cartridges were greased with pig or cow fat. To Moslems, the pig was unclean; and for a Hindu to pollute himself with the grease of a sacred cow was the most demeaning act conceivable. The sepoys saw this as but another attempt to desecrate their religion and their caste, and they flared up in revolt. Across north and central India rebel soldiers gunned down English officers, burned the company's factories, and shot their way into Delhi, where they seized the astonished puppet emperor, Bahadur Shah II, and set him firmly on the throne in an attempt to reinstate Mogul authority.

To the sepoys, this was a patriotic attempt to return India to the Indians; to the British, it was a simple case of mutiny. Thousands of troops were dispatched from England. Desperate battles were fought throughout North India, in Lucknow and Gwalior, in Delhi and Cawnpore. For more than a year the war raged on while the sepoys, who knew well the consequences of failure, fought with the abandon of martyrs. If unanimity had been established among their ranks, it is possible the rebels would have won the war. But disunion among the leaders and abysmal disorganization ultimately rendered them ineffective, and by July 1858 the mutineers had surrendered.

The results of the Sepoy Mutiny were far-reaching. The Indians now capitulated completely to foreign rule. It was, after all, no novelty for them to be under

the yoke of a foreign ruler. The English, shocked to find themselves no longer beloved masters of a docile race but hated intruders in a hostile land, abolished the East India Company and placed India under the rule of the British crown. Thousands of Her Majesty's troops were shipped east to augment the number of Britons in the sepoy army, and the finances of all British-Indian affairs were placed under the scrutiny of Parliament. Socially, the English withdrew from personal contact with the Indians and became a civilization within a civilization. By 1860, any European who consorted with "wogs," or "Westernized oriental gentlemen," was considered more than a bit eccentric.

Disdain for the native had not always existed, however, and in fact the early British traders had accommodated themselves with much willingness to the rhythms of the Hindustani world. Their families often lived in native-built houses, cooked in mud ovens, and slept on dirt floors. They ate Indian food and drank local wines, apparently with great gusto — for overeating under the tropical sun became one of the many ways of courting premature death in the Indies. Tea drinking was learned from the Indians, as was the use of the hookah, or water pipe, a pleasure enjoyed by men and women alike. Later this contraption was replaced by the less cumbersome cheroot.

In the beginning, the newcomers paid their regular respects to the Indian religions — some of His Majesty's finest were seen wearing Hindu amulets to protect against snakes and the evil eye — and to the native governments, which on particular holidays they honored with full-dress military parades. As late as 1802, British soldiers in Calcutta gave thanks for the signing of the

Treaty of Amiens by marching in front of a shrine built to the goddess Kali. Friendship between Indian and Britisher was common, and the payroll of the East India Company included employees from both worlds. Nor were such friendships confined to the factories or to one particular sex. In the early days, European women were rare in these primitive settlements (which in certain respects must have resembled nineteenth-century boom towns in the American West) and consequently, intermarriage between the races was accepted. As for those young men who cherished their bachelorhood, there was the harem, complete with servants, dancing girls, and slaves swishing peacock-tail fans. New words crept into the vernacular: bungalow, buggy, cummerbund, calico. Indian clothes, simple and cool, became popular, as did Persian wine and arrack. With little to entertain them other than gambling, conversation, the hunt, and food, the early European settlers in India wiled away the hot hours in intoxicated slumber. It was undemanding, enervating.

In all, the first colonizers were free of contempt for Indian life, and in most cases they exploited it to their most pleasurable advantage. The racial question was of little concern and relationships on both sides were cordial. Life was slow, dangerous, often prosaic, and always primitive. Yet despite the lack of amenities and the absence of Jacobean graces, there was little attempt on the part of the visitors to impose their Occidental manners on their Oriental hosts.

By the middle of the eighteenth century, when the British were no longer Mogul servants and could freely indulge in the criticisms of Indian life they had so long repressed, a new attitude of condescension emerged, and within a century this attitude evolved into the doctrine of "The White Man's Burden." Contributing to this view were the thousands of British citizens who migrated to India during the first half of the nineteenth century. This new breed, complacent and soft, was augmented by the staunch daughters of Victoria, lace-sleeved dames sternly disapproving of harems and hookahs and vociferous in their declamations of Christian duty. If the Indians had once been viewed as clever co-workers and warm companions, the newcomers were of different sentiment. By 1850, with his "idolatrous processions" and his "unmentionable rites," the poor native was thought to be a complete degenerate in need not only of social reform but also of full-scale Christian regeneration. This new posture of superiority was abetted by the governors general who followed Warren Hastings. Lord Cornwallis halted the employment of Indians in the company's offices and replaced them with Englishmen. "Every native of Hindustan," he said, "I verily believe is corrupt." He was seconded by Richard Wellesley, a staunch advocate of English supremacy. To Wellesley, the natives were unquestionably inferior — "vulgar, ignorant, rude, familiar and stupid" men. He stopped the paying of political respects to local leaders and discouraged fraternization between Indians and British. From Wellesley's administration onward this attitude continued, and the Sepoy Mutiny only confirmed the Westerner's belief in the native's turpitude. "The awful horrors of this revolt," wrote John Lourie, an American pastor, "shows us the real character of heathenism and Mohammedanism when the restraints of Providence are taken off."

The result of all this was that the English attempted

to make life in the Indian cities a duplicate of life at home in Britain. Even before the Sepoy Mutiny it was remarked by a visitor in Calcutta that "Every Briton appears to pride himself in being outrageously a John Bull," and indeed, parts of Calcutta had been transformed into an ersatz London. Lining the streets were quaint steepled churches, brownstones with chintz curtains at the windows, office buildings with classic porticos and pillared façades, and mobs of fashionably dressed British citizens riding to their appointments in hansom cabs. On holidays these good people might be found picnicking on the city mall, or at home in their parlors, gazing at pictures of Queen Victoria in gilt frames over their mantels. After business hours, the men could be found in downtown clubs, smoking cigars and playing straight-rail billiards, and the women in their drawing rooms, gossiping. "Every youth who is able to maintain a wife marries," wrote a visitor to Victorian India. "The conjugal pair become a bundle of English prejudices and hate the country, the natives and everything belonging to them. If the man has, by chance, a share of philosophy and reflection, the woman is sure to have none. Her 'odious blacks,' the 'nasty heathen wretches,' and the 'filthy creatures,' are all the shrill echoes of the 'black brutes' and the 'black vermin' of the husband."

This contempt was not confined to the natives. All products of Indian culture, by associative guilt, were condemned, and among these was architecture. From the very beginning many Britishers failed to see the value of Mogul tombs and mosques, although it must be said that in this the conquerors were following in the footsteps of the conquered. "Nothing is perma-

nent," wrote a Dutch visitor to the court of Jahangir centuries before:

> . . . yea, even the noble buildings — gardens, tombs or palaces — which, in and near every city, one cannot contemplate without pity or distress because of their ruined state. For in this they are to be despised above all the laziest nations of the world, because they build them with so many hundreds of thousands, and yet keep them in repair only so long as the owners live and have the means. Once the builder is dead, no one will care for the buildings; the son will neglect the father's work, the mother her son's, brothers and friends will take no care for each other's buildings; everyone tries, as far as possible, to erect a new building of his own, and establish his own reputation alongside that of his ancestors. Consequently, it may be said that if all these buildings and erections were attended to and repaired for a century, the lands of every city, and even village, would be adorned with monuments; but as a matter of fact the roads leading to the cities are strewn with fallen columns of stone.

Nonetheless, if the Moguls treated their architectural labors with indifference, the British at times approached them with intent to maim or destroy. The forts in Agra and Delhi were commandeered at the beginning of the nineteenth century and turned into military garrisons. Marble reliefs were torn down, gardens were trampled, and lines of ugly barracks, still standing today, were installed in their stead. In the Delhi fort, the Hall of Public Audience was made into an arsenal and the arches of the outer colonnades were bricked over or replaced with rectangular wooden windows. These insults were compounded in 1876 when, to brighten up the fort for

a visit from the Prince of Wales, the entire hall was covered with a coat of whitewash. The gardens of Sikandra were leased to British engineers for purposes of "speculative cultivation," and the Jami Masjid in Delhi, already once used as a garrison by the Sikhs, was almost transformed into a Christian cathedral; it was suggested that the names of Christian saints and martyrs should be carved into the floor. After the Sepoy Mutiny, it was even proposed that this greatest of Indian mosques be destroyed and a government building set in its place.

The Taj Mahal was not spared. By the nineteenth century, its grounds were a favorite trysting place for young Englishmen and their ladies. Open-air balls were held on the marble terrace in front of the main door, and there, beneath Shah Jahan's lotus dome, brass bands um-pah-pahed and lords and ladies danced the quadrille. The minarets became a popular site for suicide leaps, and the mosques on either side of the Taj were rented out as bungalows to honeymooners. By 1855, so many people were enjoying the delights of Mumtaz Mahal's mausoleum that a British hotel, Beaumont's, opened in Agra and advertised "refreshing and clean accommodations, and skilled natives expert at carving the following items for those who care to buy: inkstands, black stone serpents, paper cutters and marble Taj Mahals."

The gardens of the Taj were especially popular for open-air frolics. "At an earlier date, when picnic parties were held in the garden of the Taj," related Lord Curzon, a governor general in the early twentieth century, "it was not an uncommon thing for the revellers to arm themselves with hammer and chisel, with which they wiled away the afternoon by chipping out frag-

The British treated the architectural monuments of Mogul India with casual contempt. The Red Fort at Delhi (below) housed a military garrison and the Taj Mahal (left) became a public pleasure ground.

ments of agate and carnelian from the cenotaphs of the Emperor and his lamented Queen." The Taj became a place where one could drink in private, and its parks were often strewn with the figures of inebriated British soldiers. In their disrespect for the soul of the dead queen, the English were joined by mobs of careless Indians. A guidebook of 1872 noted:

> It would certainly be more in character if no festivities ever disturbed the repose of a place set aside for sacred memories; but as long as the natives hold constant fairs in the enclosure and throw orange-peels and other debris about the whole place, it is perhaps somewhat hypocritical to object to a few Englishmen refreshing themselves in a remote corner.

Scorn for native arts became so pronounced that Lord William Bentinck, who from 1828–33 served as governor general of Bengal and later became the first governor general of all India, announced his plans to demolish the best Mogul monuments in Agra and Delhi and remove their marble façades. These he intended to ship to London, where they would be broken up and sold piecemeal to members of the landed gentry who wished to embellish their estates. Several of Shah Jahan's pavilions in the Red Fort at Delhi were indeed stripped to the brick, and the marble was shipped off to England (part of this shipment included pieces for King George IV himself). Plans were then made to dismantle the Taj Mahal, and wrecking machinery was moved into the garden grounds. Just as the demolition crew was setting to work, word came from London that the first auction had been a failure and that all further sales were cancelled — it would not be worth the money to tear down the Taj Mahal.

Yet despite the ruthlessness of speculators, many British visitors were deeply struck by the beauty of the monument's design. In London, symmetrical walkways and marble fountains sprang up in parks throughout the city; white marble was more popular than ever; domes became increasingly bulbous, gardens more like Persian arabesques; on the fronts of government offices cupolas and kiosks appeared, decidedly Oriental in character, and even in America, in official buildings such as the Capitol Building of Rhode Island, an outline more than faintly reminiscent of the Taj Mahal could be discerned.

By the beginning of the 1900's there was a growing interest in Indian art, a cause Lord Curzon aided by preserving what remained of the Mogul monuments. In Delhi and Agra, more than £50,000 was spent to resuscitate ailing treasures: military units were evacuated from the forts of both cities; the tomb of Itimad-ud-Dowlah was renovated; and a multitude of marble mosques and tombs that had been turned into police stations, ticket offices, kitchens, and the like were returned to their proper uses.

Curzon especially loved the Taj Mahal. He found it in a dilapidated state and restored it to the condition it is in today. To do this, a number of native artisans were trained to cut marble and to repair mosaics and were put to work replacing the stones that had been plucked and hacked away by souvenir hunters. They patched the cracks in the minarets caused by an earthquake in the early part of the nineteenth century, and they polished the dingy marble walls. The stone channels were dug out, flower beds and avenues of trees were replanted, water from the Jumna River was once again circulated through the fountains. Finally, in Curzon's words, the Taj was:

. . . no longer approached through dust wastes and squalid bazaars. A beautiful park takes their place; and the group of mosques and tombs, the arcaded streets and the grassy courts that precede the main buildings, are once more as nearly as possible what they were when completed by the masons of Shah Jahan. Every building in the garden enclosure of the Taj has been scrupulously repaired, and the discovery of old plans has enabled us to restore the water channels and flower beds in the garden more exactly to their original state.

After overhauling the walls and walkways of the Taj, Lord Curzon wished to embellish its interior with a beautiful hanging lamp. Not able to locate a metal worker in India with enough skill to fashion such a lamp, he commissioned the work in Cairo, where a hanging brass lantern modeled on one that hung in an ancient Egyptian mosque was produced. In the first decade of the twentieth century, this lamp was installed in the tomb and it hangs there today, suspended from the interior central dome. Curzon was pleased with his work: "The central dome of the Taj is rising like some vast exhalation into the air," he proclaimed in a speech given on the terrace of the Taj Mahal, "and on the other side the red rampart of the Fort stands like a crimson barricade against the sky. . . . If I had never done anything else in India, I have written my name here, and the letters are a living joy."

Curzon was not the only foreigner smitten with the Taj Mahal. Despite neglect and the marble merchant's sinister designs, it had fascinated visitors since the days

of Bernier and Tavernier. By the beginning of the twentieth century, the Taj was already an overworked subject for poems and paintings, was a popular topic for travel stories, and the recipient of voluminous pages of praise. Rudyard Kipling called it "The ivory gate through which all good dreams pass." "Henceforth, let the inhabitants of the world be divided into two classes," suggested the writer Edward Lear, "— them as has seen the Taj Mahal; and them as hasn't." A famous British architect, Sir Edwin Lutyens, exclaimed that "It is wonderful but not architecture, and its beauty begins where architecture ceases to be." Edward, Prince of Wales, was similarly eloquent: "Many writers who have tried their hands at a description of the Taj," he wrote, "set out with the admission that it is indescribable, and then proceed to give some idea of it." Perhaps most dramatic of all such utterances came from the wife of Major W. H. Sleeman, the man who championed Austin de Bordeaux as designer of the Taj. "I cannot tell you what I think for I know not how to criticize such a building," she said, "but I can tell you what I feel. I would die tomorrow to have such another over me."

Since Mrs. Sleeman's time the Taj has become perhaps the most universally appreciated building in the world, and no doubt there are those who would still die tomorrow to lie beneath its dome. Yet, despite the worldwide encomiums it has received, the Taj essentially belongs to India. In the land of Hindustan there is scarcely a schoolboy who does not know the story of Mumtaz Mahal, scarcely a bootblack or beggar who does not dream of visiting her tomb. At the same time, this building no longer belongs to the Moguls, nor to an empire, nor to a handsome king and beautiful queen who died so many years ago. Today it is the possession of all the Indian people, and these crowd its gates every hour, some with cameras, some in groups of laughing tourists, some on their knees in prayer. All of India salutes the Taj Mahal, and love for this building is perhaps the one thing that all Indians have in common. In a country like India, a country divided by so many religions and so many tongues, it is a bow to the power of art that a work like the Taj Mahal is capable of creating the unanimity that man and his many policies have failed to achieve; and one suspects that even this was part of the plan foreseen by those unknown geniuses who carved its stones.

THE TAJ MAHAL
IN LITERATURE

Nine nineteenth-century engravings illustrate The Taj Mahal in Literature *(pages 138–57). Above is a view of the Taj Mahal from the banks of the Jumna River.*

EARLY VISITORS FROM FRANCE

Only a few Western visitors reached the court of the Great Moguls in India during the seventeenth century. One of the earliest to come was Jean Baptiste Tavernier, a French jewel merchant, whose arrival in Agra in 1641 coincided with the construction of the Taj Mahal.

Agra . . . is the largest town in India, and was formerly the residence of the Kings. The houses of the nobles are beautiful and well built, but those of private persons have nothing fine about them, no more than in all the other towns of India. They are separated from one another, and are concealed by the height of the walls, from fear lest any one should see the women; so it is easy to understand that all these towns have nothing cheerful about them like our towns in Europe. It should be added to this that, Agra being surrounded by sands, the heat in summer is excessive, and it is, in part, this which induced Sháh Jahán not to make his ordinary dwelling there any more, and to remove his court to Jahánábád. . . .

Of all the tombs which one sees at Agra, that of the wife of Sháh Jahán is the most splendid. He purposely made it near the Tasimacan, where all foreigners come, so that the whole world should see and admire its magnificence. The Tasimacan is a large bazaar, consisting of six large courts all surrounded with porticoes, under which there are chambers for the use of merchants, and an enormous quantity of cottons is sold there. The tomb of this *Begum,* or sultan queen, is at the east end of the town by the side of the river in a great square surrounded by walls, upon which there is a small gallery, as on the walls of many towns in Europe. This square is a kind of garden divided into compartments like our parterres, but in the places where we put gravel there is white and black marble. You enter this square by a large gate, and at first you see, on the left hand, a beautiful gallery which faces in the direction of Mecca, where there are three or four niches where the *Moufti* comes at fixed times to pray. A little farther than the middle of the square, on the side of the water, you see three great platforms elevated, one upon the other, with four towers at the four corners of each, and a staircase inside, for proclaiming the hour of prayer. There is a dome above, which is scarcely less magnificent than that of Val de Grace at Paris. It is covered within and without with white marble, the middle being of brick. Under this dome there is an empty tomb, for the *Begum* is interred under a vault which is beneath the first platform. The same changes which are made below in this subterranean place are made above around the tomb, for from time to time they change the carpet, chandeliers, and other ornaments of that kind, and there are always there some *Mollahs* to pray. I witnessed the commencement and accomplishment of this great work, on which they have expended twenty-two years, during which twenty thousand men worked incessantly; this is sufficient to enable one to realise that the cost of it has been enormous. It is said that the scaffoldings alone cost more than the entire work, because, from want of wood, they had all to be made of brick, as well as the supports of the arches; this has entailed much labour and a heavy expenditure. Sháh Jahán began to build his own tomb on the other side of the river, but the war which he had with his sons interrupted his plan, and Aurangzeb, who reigns at present, is not disposed to complete it. An eunuch in command of 2000 men guards both the tomb of the *Begum* and the Tasimacan, to which it is near at hand.

JEAN BAPTISTE TAVERNIER
Travels in India, 1676

On a later trip to India, Tavernier was accompanied by François Bernier, a noted French physician. Sharply critical of Indian polity and customs, Bernier reported on the unexpected charm of Agra's chief monument in this letter to his patron, Jean Baptiste Colbert, Louis XIV's powerful finance minister.

I shall finish this letter with a description of the two wonderful mausoleums which constitute the chief superiority of *Agra* over *Delhi*. One was erected by *Jehan-Guyre* in honour of his father *Ekbar;* and *Chah-Jehan* raised the other to the memory of his wife *Tage Mehale,* that extraordinary and celebrated beauty, of whom her husband was so enamoured that it is said he was constant to her during life, and at her death was so affected as nearly to follow her to the grave.

I shall pass *Ekbar's* monument without further observation, because all its beauties are found in still greater perfection in that of *Tage Mehale.* . . .

On leaving *Agra,* toward the east, you enter a long, wide, or paved street, on a gentle ascent, having on one side a high and long wall, which forms the side of a square garden, of much greater extent than our *Place Royale,* and on the other side a row of new houses with arcades, resembling those of the principal streets in *Dehli* . . . . After walking half the length of the wall, you find on the right, that is, on the side of the houses, a large gate, tolerably well made, which is the entrance of a *Karvan-Serrah,* and on the opposite side from that of the wall is seen the magnificent gate of a spacious and square pavilion, forming the entrance into the garden, between two reservoirs, faced with hewn stone.

This pavilion is an oblong square, and built of a stone resembling red marble, but not so hard. The front seems to me longer, and much more grand in its construction, than that of *S. Louis,* in the rue *S. Antoine,* and it is equally lofty. The columns, the architraves and the cornices are, indeed, not formed according to the proportion of the five orders of architecture so strictly observed in *French* edifices. The building I am speaking of is of a different and peculiar kind; but not without something pleasing in its whimsical structure; and in my opinion it well deserves a place in our books of architecture. It consists almost wholly of arches upon arches, and galleries upon galleries, disposed and contrived in an hundred different ways. Nevertheless the edifice has a magnificent appearance, and is conceived and executed effectually. Nothing offends the eye; on the contrary, it is delighted with every part, and never tired with looking. The last time I visited *Tage Mehale's* mausoleum I was in the company of a French merchant [Tavernier], who, as well as myself, thought that this extraordinary fabric could not be sufficiently admired. I did not venture to express my opinion, fearing that my taste might have become corrupted by my long residence in the *Indies;* and as my companion was come recently from *France,* it was quite a relief to my mind to hear him say that he had seen nothing in *Europe* so bold and majestic.

When you have entered a little way into the pavilion approaching toward the garden, you find yourself under a lofty cupola, surrounded above with galleries, and having two divans or platforms below, one on the right, the other on the left. . . .

When at the end of the principal walk or terrace, besides the dome that faces you, are discovered two large pavilions, one to the right, another to the left, both built with the same kind of stone, consequently of the same red colour as the first pavilion. These are spacious square edifices, the parts

Akbar's tomb at Sikandra

of which are raised over each other in the form of balconies and terraces; three arches have openings which have the garden wall for a boundary, and you walk under these pavilions as if they were lofty and wide galleries. I shall not stop to speak of the interior ornaments of the two pavilions, because they scarcely differ in regard to the walls, ceiling, or pavement from the dome which I am going to describe. Between the end of the principal walk and this dome is an open and pretty large space, which I call a water-parterre, because the stones on which you walk, cut and figured in various forms, represent the borders of box in our parterres. From the middle of this space you have a good view of the building which contains the tomb. . . .

This building is a vast dome of white marble nearly of the same height as the *Val De Grace* of *Paris,* and encircled by a number of turrets, also of white marble, descending the one below the other in regular succession. The whole fabric is supported by four great arches, three of which are quite open and the other closed up by the wall of an apartment with a gallery attached to it. There the *Koran* is continually read with apparent devotion in respectful memory of *Tage Mehale* by certain *Mullahs* kept in the mausoleum for that purpose. The centre of every arch is adorned with white marble slabs whereon are inscribed large *Arabian* characters in black marble, which produce a fine effect. The interior or concave part of the dome and generally the whole of the wall from top to bottom are faced with white marble: no part can be found that is not skilfully wrought, or that has not its peculiar beauty. Everywhere are seen the jasper, and *jachen,* or jade, as well as other stones similar to those that enrich the walls of the *Grand Duke's* chapel at *Florence,* and several more of great value and rarity, set in an endless variety of modes, mixed and enchased in the slabs of marble which face the body of the wall. Even the squares of white and black marble which compose the pavement are inlaid with these precious stones in the most beautiful and delicate manner imaginable.

Under the dome is a small chamber, wherein is enclosed the tomb of *Tage Mehale.* It is opened with much ceremony once in a year, and once only; and as no Christian is admitted within, lest its sanctity should be profaned, I have not seen the interior, but I understand that nothing can be conceived more rich and magnificent.

It only remains to draw your attention to a walk or terrace, nearly five-and-twenty paces in breadth and rather more in height, which runs from the dome to the extremity of the garden. From this terrace are seen the *Gemna* flowing below, a large expanse of luxuriant gardens, a part of the city of *Agra,* the fortress, and all the fine residences of the *Omrahs* erected on the banks of the river. When I add that this terrace extends almost the whole length of one side of the garden, I leave you to judge whether I had not sufficient ground for asserting that the mausoleum of *Tage Mehale* is an astonishing work. It is possible I may have imbibed an Indian taste; but I decidedly think that this monument deserves much more to be numbered among the wonders of the world than the pyramids of *Egypt,* those unshapen masses which when I had seen them twice yielded me no satisfaction, and which are nothing on the outside but heaps of large stones piled in the form of steps one upon another, while within there is very little that is creditable either to human skill or to human invention.

FRANÇOIS BERNIER
Travels in the Mogul Empire, 1670

141

Within a century after Shah Jahan built the Taj Mahal as a memorial to his queen, his Mogul successors were rulers of India in name only. The disintegration of the empire had followed rapidly upon the death of Shah Jahan's son, Aurangzeb, in 1707: native Hindu princes declared their independence from the central government, while the commercial and political power of the British East India Company increased. But the lure of the Taj Mahal continued to grip even such stolid types as British army officers. W. H. Sleeman, an able administrator in the Bengal army who was instrumental in suppressing the thuggees—semireligious gangs of professional assassins who plagued Indian society—fulfilled a lifelong dream when he visited the tomb in 1836.

On the 1st of January, 1836, we went on sixteen miles to Agra, and when within about six miles of the city, the dome and minaret of the Taj opened upon us from behind a small grove of fruit trees, close by us on the side of the road. The morning was not clear, but it was a good one for a first sight of this building, which appeared larger through the dusty haze than it would have done through a clear sky. For five and twenty years of my life had I been looking forward to the sight now before me. Of no building on earth had I heard so much as of this, which contains the remains of the Emperor Shah Jehan, and his wife. . . . We had ordered our tents to be pitched in the gardens of this splendid mausoleum, that we might have our full of the enjoyment which everybody seemed to derive from it; and we reached them about eight o'clock. I went over the whole building before I entered my tent; and from the first sight of the dome and minarets on the distant horizon, to the last glance back from my tent-ropes to the magnificent gateway that forms the entrance from our camp to the quadrangle in which they stand, I can truly say that everything surpassed my expectations. I at first thought the dome formed too large a portion of the whole building; that its neck was too long and too much exposed; and that the minarets were too plain in their design; but after going repeatedly over every part, and examining the *tout ensemble* from all possible positions, and in all possible lights, from that of the full moon at midnight in a cloudless sky, to that of the noon-day sun, the mind seemed to repose in the calm persuasion, that there was an entire harmony of parts, a faultless congregation of architectural beauties, on which it could dwell for ever without fatigue.

After my quarter of a century of anticipated pleasure, I went on from part to part in the expectation that I must by-and-by come to something that would disappoint me; but no, the emotion which one feels at first is never impaired: on the contrary, it goes on improving from the first *coup d'oeil* of the dome in the distance, to the minute inspection of the last flower upon the screen round the tomb. One returns and returns to it with undiminished pleasure; and though at every return one's attention to the smaller parts becomes less and less, the pleasure which he derives from the contemplation of the greater, and of the whole collectively, seems to increase; and he leaves it with a feeling of regret, that he could not have it all his life within his reach; and of assurance that the image of what he has seen can never be obliterated from his mind "while memory holds her seat." I felt that it was to me in architecture what Kemble and his sister, Mrs. Siddons, had been to me a quarter of a century before in acting, something that must stand alone — something that I should never cease to see clearly in my mind's eye, and yet never be able clearly to describe to others.

The Emperor and his Queen lie buried side by side in a vault beneath the building, to which we descend by a flight of steps. Their remains are covered by two slabs of marble; and directly over these slabs, upon the floor above, in the great centre room under the dome, stand two other slabs, or cenotaphs, of the same marble exquisitely worked in mosaic. Upon that of the Queen, amid wreaths of flowers, are worked in black letters passages from the Koran; one of which, at the end facing the entrance, terminates with, "And defend us from the *tribe* of unbelievers;" that very *tribe* which are now gathered from all quarters of the civilized world, to admire the splendour of the tomb which was raised to perpetuate her name. On the slab over her husband, there are no passages from the Koran; merely mosaic work of flowers, with his name, and the date of his death. I asked some of the learned Mahomedan attendants, the cause of this difference; and was told, that Shah Jehan had himself designed the slab over his wife, and saw no harm in inscribing the *words of God* upon it; but that the slab over himself was designed by his more pious son, Ourungzebe, who did not think it right to place these *holy words* upon a stone which the foot of man might some day touch, though that stone covered the remains of his own father. . . .

The building stands upon the north side of a large quadrangle, looking down into the clear blue stream of the river Jumna, while the other three sides are enclosed with a high wall of red sandstone. The entrance to this quadrangle is through a magnificent gateway in the south side opposite the tomb; and on the other two sides are very beautiful mosques facing inwards, and corresponding exactly with each other in size, design, and execution. That on the left or west side, is the only one that can be used as a mosque or church; because the faces of the audience, and those of all men at their prayers, must be turned towards the tomb of their prophet to the west. The pulpit is always against the dead wall at the back, and the audience face towards it, standing with their backs to the open front of the building. The church on the east side is used for the accommodation of visitors, or for any secular purpose; and was built merely as a *jowab* (answer) to the real one. The whole area is laid out in square parterres, planted with flowers and shrubs in the centre, and with fine trees, chiefly the cypress, all round the borders, forming an avenue to every road. These roads are all paved with slabs of freestone, and have, running along the centre, a basin, with a row of jets d'eau in the middle from one extremity to the other. These are made to play almost every evening, when the gardens are much frequented by the European gentlemen and ladies of the station, and by natives of all religions and sects. The quadrangle is from east to west nine hundred and sixty-four feet; and from north to south three hundred and twenty-nine.

The mausoleum itself, the terrace upon which it stands, and the minarets, are all formed of the finest white marble inlaid with precious stones. The wall around the quadrangle, including the river face of the terrace, is made of red sandstone, with cupolas and pillars of the same white marble. The inside of the churches and apartments in and upon the walls are all lined with marble or with stucco work that looks like marble; but on the outside, the red sandstone resembles uncovered bricks. The dazzling white marble of the mausoleum itself rising over the red wall, is apt, at first sight, to make a disagreeable impression, from the idea of a whitewashed head to an unfinished building; but this impression is very soon removed, and tends perhaps to improve that which is afterwards received from a nearer inspection. The marble was all brought from the Jeypore territories upon wheeled carriages, a distance, I believe, of two or three hundred miles; and the sandstone from the neighbourhood of Dholepore and Futtehpore Secree. Shah Jehan is said to have inherited his partiality for this colour from his grandfather, Akbar, who constructed almost all his buildings from the same stone, though he might have had the beautiful white freestone at the same cost. What was figuratively said of Augustus may be most literally said of Shah Jehan: he found the cities (Agra and Delhi) all brick, and left them all marble; for all the marble buildings, and additions to buildings, were formed by him. . . .

We were encamped upon a fine green sward outside the entrance to the south, in a kind of large court, enclosed by a high cloistered wall, in which all our attendants and followers found shelter. Colonel and Mrs. King, and some other gentlemen, were encamped in the same place, and for the same purpose; and we had a very agreeable party. The band of our friend Major Godby's regiment played sometimes in the evening upon the terrace of the Taj; but of all the complicated music ever heard upon earth, that of a flute blown gently in the vault below, where the remains of the Emperor and his consort repose, as the sound rises to the dome amidst a hundred arched alcoves around, and descends in heavenly reverberations upon those who sit or recline upon the cenotaphs above the vault, is perhaps the finest to an inartificial ear. We feel as if it were from heaven, and breathed by angels; it is to the ear what the building itself is to the eye; but unhappily it cannot, like the building, live in our recollections. All that we can, in after life, remember is, that it was heavenly, and produced heavenly emotions.

W. H. SLEEMAN
Rambles and Recollections of an Indian Official, 1844

Fatehpur Sikri

During the early nineteenth century, the British consolidated their control over the Indian subcontinent against immense odds and at the price of frequent military maneuvers. Adventurers and mercenaries were naturally attracted by the resulting opportunity for gainful employment in India. One such gentleman was Leopold von Orlich. A captain in the German army, he had hoped to participate in the Anglo-Afghan war in the Kabul but arrived too late. Instead, he undertook a peaceful tour of the Indian countryside.

My first excursion was to the Tauje Mahal, or the Diamond of Seraglios, the most beautiful edifice in India. It is situated a mile to the south of the city, close to the Jumna, and was built by the emperor Shah Jehan, in honour of his beloved consort Mumtaz Mahal. . . .

We rode along the bank of the river by a road made during the famine in 1838, and passed the ruins of the palaces in which the nobles resided during the reign of Akbar the Great. Here are walls so colossal and solid, that they are preserved in spite of all the violence which they have suffered: we saw pieces ten feet thick united by a cement which nothing but gunpowder can break up.

We perceived at a considerable distance this diamond of the buildings of the world, which from the dazzling whiteness of the marble, of which this magnificent sepulchre is built, looks like an enchanted castle of burnished silver. It is a lofty dome, surrounded by four minarets 120 feet in height, and of such admirable workmanship, that the whole is in perfect preservation;

except that a few crevices were caused by the earthquake in 1803, which have, however, been carefully filled up with cement. We entered on the east side through a lofty vaulted gate, adorned with mosaics, into the exterior court, which is enclosed by a high wall of red sandstone with four bronze doors: the four corners are flanked by bastions, which serve as the bases of octagon buildings, which are crowned by lofty domes supported by angular pillars. Here were the dwellings of the keepers, and the apartments assigned to the reception of travellers who visited this wonderful edifice. On the south side is a second gate, still more beautiful and massive, and leading to the garden, which is enclosed by high walls.

An avenue of ancient cypresses, between which are marble basins, fountains, and flower-beds, leads in a direct line to a broad flight of marble steps; by this we ascended to a spacious platform; above which rises the noble dome, with its elegant slender minarets. The garden is always filled with fragrant flowers, and is intended to represent eternal spring; and the wanderer finds protection against the scorching rays of the sun, under the shade of the tamarinds, banyan, fig, and mango trees.

The Tauje Mahal forms an octagon which supports a cupola seventy feet in diameter, adorned with arabesques and garlands of flowers, in the style of Florentine mosaic. The interior consists of an immense vault, which is lighted from above, by marble windows of lattice work, and is surrounded on the four principal sides by as many vaulted vestibules. It is covered with mosaic of the most splendid precious stones, which, conformably to the idea of paradise in the Koran, ornaments the walls like an arbour of the most tasteful and manifold festoons of flowers and fruits of every kind; even sounds, as they gradually die away in these magic halls, resemble the music of an expiring echo. In one of the most beautiful of these flowers there are seventy-two precious stones: in the mosaic, twelve kinds of stone are chiefly employed; among which are lapis lazuli, agate, cornelian, blood-red jasper, chalcedony, sardonyx, &c. The first, not found in India, is said to have been brought from Tibet. . . .

From the left side of the principal entrance, sacrilegious hands had stolen a few of the most valuable stones out of the mosaic; but the British government has had the place repaired under the direction of Captain Boileau, and paid 3000 rupees for the restoration of these few arabesques! Keepers and gardeners are now appointed, and on Sundays the fountains play, and hundreds of people visit the spot. The minarets stand detached at each corner, scarcely twenty paces from the main building. They have within, a winding staircase of 162 steps, which leads to the very summit. . . .

The finest prospect is from the upper gallery of the south-east minaret, and from that point I have seen not only the rising and setting of the sun, but also this fairy palace illuminated by the bright light of the moon. At these times, the most solemn silence prevails: the air is more filled than ever with the aromatic perfume of the flowers, and a magic glow is shed over the wondrous building. The Jumna meanders, like a stream of silver, through the verdant landscape; the ruins of palaces and sepulchres cast a mysterious shade; and Agra, with its minarets and elegant marble palaces in the boldly rising citadel, seems to be shrouded in a mystic veil, under which the numerous lights of the strand and the bazars sparkle like little stars.

LEOPOLD VON ORLICH
Travels in India, 1845

American military men, no less than European, were attracted to India. Robert Ogden Tyler, a brevet major general in the Union army during the American Civil War, spent several months there in 1873 following his retirement.

I have tried to give you a faithful account of our lives, and what passed before our eyes from day to day. I have avoided guide-books, and have not done your extensive reading the injustice of trying to pass off as my own, extracts from those who have written better and more fully on the same topics. I feel that I ought to beg pardon for the lack of incident and adventure. When advised to seek opportunities to hunt the wild beasts of India, I have declined on the ground that I have no quarrel with the animals, as they have never injured either my relatives or myself. I have also pleaded lack of practice. . . .

We have avoided rather than sought colonial society. . . .

Daylight disclosed to us a country dry and barren except where irrigated, on which the saleratus-patches, ground-squirrels, and occasional herds of antelope reminded us of the Humboldt Valley. At Toondla Junction, about eleven o'clock, we took the usual branch line for Agra, and it was not long before we saw the dome of the Taj looming up through the dust-laden air. Like the dome of our Capitol at Washington, that of St. Peter's at Rome, or the Mosque of the citadel at Cairo, the white, glittering structure of the Taj seems to form the centre of the landscape from every point of view. *Faute de mieux*, we took billet at Beaumont's, a hotel of past reputation, which has now fallen into especially incompetent hands. An Englishman and wife, and a roving Boston gentleman named M———, are, beside ourselves, the only guests. The night was balmy, the moon bright, and, as it is the correct thing to do, we Americans drove together to the Taj. Alighting at the grand gateway and ascending a few steps, we saw through the arches, and at the end of the vista, that marvelous pile of marble, the most beautiful tribute ever paid by man to the memory of a beloved wife. The first view shows its beauty, but time and study are required to take in the perfection of the work. The tomb and its surroundings occupy three terraces. The first is a beautiful garden, which the government has the good taste to keep in perfect order. An avenue of trees, with a long reservoir down the middle, full of fountains, stretches in charming perspective from the gate to the building. Similar avenues cross the main one, and the view at the end of each is closed by some appropriate piece of architecture. The second terrace is of red sandstone, on the front of which is the river Jumna, and at either end are two mosques precisely similar, of which one is styled the *answer* to the other. The third terrace is all of white marble, and includes the tomb and the minarets at the four corners of the plateau. Seen by moonlight, the darker inlaid-work and the discoloration disappear, and all is pure white. The lines and tracery are softened and blended, and it seems so delicate and intangible that one would hardly be surprised if at some moment it should melt like a cloud into "thin air." After having sufficiently contemplated the moonlight scene, we went into the interior, which had been illuminated by blue-lights. This gave a distinctness and beauty to the walls, the inside, the dome, and the lace-like marble screen surrounding the central mosaic-inlaid memorials of Nour-Jehan and her husband, such as no daylight can produce.

ROBERT OGDEN TYLER
Memoir, 1873

Palace of Agra

POETS' DELIGHT

The breadth of the traditional grand tour was expanded during the nineteenth century to include the more exotic East. Bayard Taylor, an American novelist and journalist, followed up a walking tour of Europe with a stint as historian on Commodore Matthew Perry's successful naval expedition that led to the opening of Japan. In the 1850's he also visited India.

The Taj is built on the bank of the Jumna, rather more than a mile to the eastward of the Fort of Agra. It is approached by a handsome road, cut through the mounds left by the ruins of ancient palaces. Like the tomb of Akbar, it stands in a large garden, inclosed by a lofty wall of red sandstone, with arched galleries around the interior. The entrance is a superb gateway of sandstone, inlaid with ornaments and inscriptions from the Koran, in white marble. Outside of this grand portal, however, is a spacious quadrangle of solid masonry, with an elegant structure intended as a caravanserai, on the opposite side. Whatever may be the visitor's impatience, he cannot help pausing to notice the fine proportions of these structures, and the rich and massive style of their architecture. The gate to the garden of the Taj is not so large as that of Akbar's tomb, but quite as beautiful in design. Passing under the open demi-vault, whose arch hangs high above you, an avenue of dark Italian cypresses appears before you. Down its centre sparkles a long row of fountains, each casting up a single slender jet. On both sides, the palm, the banyan, and the feathery bamboo mingle their foliage; the song of birds meets your ear, and the odor of roses and lemon-flowers sweetens the air. Down such a vista, and over such a foreground, rises the Taj.

It is an octagonal building, or rather, a square with the corners truncated, and each side precisely similar. It stands upon a lofty platform, or pedestal, with a minaret at each corner, and this, again, is lifted on a vast terrace of solid masonry. An Oriental dome, swelling out boldly from the base into nearly two-thirds of a sphere, and tapering at the top into a crescent-tipped spire, crowns the edifice, rising from its centre, with four similar, though much smaller domes, at the corners. On each side there is a grand entrance, formed by a single pointed arch, rising nearly to the cornice, and two smaller arches (one placed above the other) on either hand. The height of the building, from its base to the top of the dome, is 262 feet, and of the minarets, about 200 feet. But no words can convey an idea of the exquisite harmony of the different parts, and the grand and glorious effect of the whole structure, with its attendant minarets.

The material is of the purest white marble, little inferior to that of Carrara. It shines so dazzlingly in the sun, that you can scarcely look at it near at hand, except in the morning and evening. Every part — even the basement, the dome, and the upper galleries of the minarets — is inlaid with ornamental designs in marble of different colors, principally a pale brown, and a bluish violet variety. Great as are the dimensions of the Taj, it is as laboriously finished as one of those Chinese caskets of ivory and ebony, which are now so common in Europe. . . . Around all the arches of the portals and the windows — around the cornice and the domes — on the walls and in the passages, are inlaid chapters of the Koran, the letters being exquisitely formed of black marble. It is asserted that the whole of the Koran is thus inlaid, in the Taj, and I can readily believe it to be true. The building is perfect in every part. Any dilapidations it may have suffered are so well restored that all traces of them have disappeared.

I ascended to the base of the building — a gleaming marble platform, almost on a level with the tops of the trees in the garden. Before entering the central hall, I descended to the vault where the beautiful Noor-Jehan is buried. A sloping passage, the walls and floor of which have been so polished by the hands and feet of thousands, that you must walk carefully to avoid sliding down, conducts to a spacious vaulted chamber. There is no light but what enters the door, and this falls directly upon the tomb of the Queen in the centre. Shah-Jehan, whose ashes are covered by a simpler cenotaph, raised somewhat above hers, sleeps by her side. The vault was filled with the odors of rose, jasmine, and sandal-wood, the precious attars of which are sprinkled upon the tomb. Wreaths of beautiful flowers lay upon it, or withered around its base.

These were the true tombs, the monuments for display being placed in the grand hall above, which is a lofty rotunda, lighted both from above and below by screens of marble, wrought in filigree. It is paved with blocks of white marble and jasper, and ornamented with a wainscoting of sculptured tablets, representing flowers. The tombs are sarcophagi of the purest marble, exquisitely inlaid with blood-stone, agate, cornelian, lapis-lazuli, and other precious stones, and surrounded with an octagonal screen six feet high, in the open tracery of which lilies, irises, and other flowers are interwrought with the most intricate ornamental designs. This is also a marble, covered with precious stones. From the resemblance of this screen and the workmanship of the tomb to Florentine mosaic, it is supposed by some to have been executed by an Italian artist; and I have even heard it stated that the Taj was designed by an Italian architect. One look at the Taj ought to assure any intelligent man that this is false — nay, impossible, from the very nature of the thing. The Taj is the purest Saracenic, in form, proportions, and ornamental designs. If that were not sufficient, we have still the name of the Moslem architect, sculptured upon the building. . . .

Tomb of Itimad-ud-Dowlah in Agra

The Taj truly is, as I have already said, a poem. It is not only a pure architectural type, but also a creation which satisfies the imagination, because its characteristic is Beauty. Did you ever build a Castle in the Air? Here is one, brought down to earth, and fixed for the wonder of ages; yet so light it seems, so airy, and, when seen from a distance, so like a fabric of mist and sunbeams, with its great dome soaring up, a silvery bubble, about to burst in the sun, that, even after you have touched it, and climbed to its summit, you almost doubt its reality. The four minarets which surround it are perfect — no other epithet will describe them. You cannot conceive of their proportions being changed in any way, without damage to the general effect. On one side of the Taj is a mosque with three domes, of red sandstone, covered with mosaic of white marble. Now, on the opposite side, there is a building precisely similar, but of no use whatever, except as a balance to the mosque, lest the perfect symmetry of the whole design should be spoiled. This building is called the *jowàb*, or "answer." Nothing can better illustrate the feeling for proportion which prevailed in those days — and proportion is Art.

But the sun grows hot; it is nearly noon. We have spent three hours in and around the Taj, and we must leave it. Nothing that is beautiful can be given up without a pang, but if a man would travel, he must endure many such partings.

BAYARD TAYLOR
A Visit to India, China and Japan, 1855

Edward Lear's fame rests primarily on his A Book of Nonsense *and other volumes of humorous verse that popularized the whimsical limerick — everyone is familiar with his classic* The Owl and the Pussycat. *But Lear's lifelong ambition was to achieve recognition as a serious landscape painter and, toward that end, he traveled around the world with a sketchbook, publishing illustrated accounts of his many journeys. One such trip in 1874 led the Englishman to visit India and, in due course, the fabled Taj Mahal.*

February 15

This journey from Allahabad to Agra has not been by any means so terrible as I had foreshadowed it. From some cause or another, I got more or less sleep, nor had I, as generally, cramps over certain other railway-created miseries. The Taj Mahal, as you approach the fort, seems to be on the opposite side of the river, owing to the Jumna winding so much; the fort looks to be a wondrous specimen of Mogul architecture. Beyond these things, threading a line of very dirty bazaars, we get to a bungalow standing in a small compound, styled Harrison's Tourist's Hotel and after a wash, and some food, set off to see the Taj. This perfect and most lovely building infinitely surpassed all I had expected, principally on account of its size, and its colour. It is quite impossible to imagine a more beautiful or wonderful sight. Afterwards I went to the fort, and all about the building there, with which I was delighted and astonished beyond expression, particularly with the view of the river Jumna and of the Taj Mahal from the ramparts, or rather battlements. The colouring of Agra is amazingly beautiful. But I grew tired.

February 16

Came to the Taj Mahal; descriptions of this wonderfully lovely place are simply silly, as no words can describe it at all. What a garden! What flowers! What gorgeously dressed and be-ringed women; some of them very good-looking too, and all well clothed though apparently poor. Men, mostly in white, some with red shawls, some quite dressed in red, or red-brown; orange, yellow, scarlet, or purple shawls, or white; effects of colour absolutely astonishing, the great centre of the picture being ever the vast glittering ivory-white Taj Mahal, and the accompaniment and contrast of the dark green of cypresses, with the rich yellow green trees of all sorts! And then the effect of the innumerable flights of bright green parrots flitting across like live emeralds; and of the scarlet poinciannas and countless other flowers beaming bright off the dark green! The tinker or tinpot bird ever at work; pigeons, hoopoes and, I think, a new sort of mynah, pale dove colour and gray; also squirrels, and all tame, and endlessly numerous. Poinsettias are in huge crimson masses, and the purple flowered bougainvillaea runs up the cypress trees. Aloes also, and some new sort of fern or palm, I don't know which. The garden is indescribable. Below the Taj Mahal is a scene of pilgrim-washing and shrines, altogether Indian and lovely. What can I do here? Certainly not the architecture, which I naturally shall not attempt, except perhaps in a slight sketch of one of two direct garden views. Henceforth, let the inhabitants of the world be divided into two classes — them as has seen the Taj Mahal; and them as hasn't.

EDWARD LEAR
Indian Journal, 1874

A deep reverence for Indian culture drew Sir Edwin Arnold, the English poet and journalist, to the Taj Mahal in the late nineteenth century. A student of Oriental languages, he is best known for his lyrical translations of The Indian Song of Songs *and* Indian Idylls.

Aurangzeb's tomb in Khuldabad

In truth, it is difficult to speak of what has been so often described, the charm of which remains nevertheless quite indescribable. As a matter of course, our first hours in Agra were devoted to contemplation of that tender elegy in marble, which by its beauty has made immortal the loveliness that it commemorates. The Tartar princes and princesses from whom sprang the proud line of the Moguls were wont in their lifetime to choose a piece of picturesque ground, to enclose it with high walls, embellish its precincts with flower-beds and groves of shady trees, and to build upon it a *Bara-duri*, a "twelve-gated" Pleasure House, where they took delight during the founder's life. When he died the pavilion became a mausoleum, and never again echoed with song and music. Perhaps the fair daughter of Asuf-Khan, Shah Jehan's Sultana, had loved this very garden in her life. . . .

In all the world no queen had ever such a monument. You have read a thousand times all about the Taj; you know exactly — so you believe — what to expect. There will be the gateway of red sandstone with the embroidered sentences upon it from the "Holy Book," the demi-vault inlaid with flowers and scrolls, then the green garden opening a long vista over marble pavements, between masses of heavy foliage and mournful pillars of the cypress, ranged like sentinels to guard the solemnity of the spot. At the far end of this vista, beyond the fountains and the marble platform, amid four stately white towers, you know what sweet and symmetrical dome will be beheld, higher than its breadth, solid and majestic, but yet soft and delicate in its swelling proportions and its milk-white sheen. Prepared to admire, you are also aware of the defects alleged against the Taj — the rigidity of its outlines, the lack of shadow upon its unbroken front and flanks, and the coloured inlaying said to make it less a triumph of architecture than a Mosaic work, an illustration somewhat too striking and lavish of what is declared of the Moguls, that they "designed like giants, and finished like jewellers." You determine to judge it dispassionately, not carried away by the remembrance that twenty thousand workmen were employed for twenty-two years in its construction, that it cost hard upon two million pounds sterling, and that gems and precious stones came in camel-loads from all parts of the earth to furnish the inlayers with their material. Then you pass beneath the stately portal — in itself sufficient to commemorate the proudest of princesses — and as the white cupola of the Taj rises before the gaze and reveals its beauty — grace by grace — as you pace along the pavemented avenue, the mind refuses to criticise what enchants the eye and fills the heart with a sentiment of reverence for the royal love which could thus translate itself into alabaster. If it be time of sunlight the day is softened to perpetual afternoon by the shadows cast from the palms and peepuls, the thuja trees, and the pomegranates, while the hot wind is cooled by the scent of roses and jasmine. If it be moonlight, the dark avenue leads the gaze mysteriously to the soft and lofty splendour of that dome. In either case, when the first platform is reached, and the full glory of this snow-white wonder comes into sight, one can no more stay to criticise its details than to analyse a beautiful face suddenly seen. Admiration, delight, astonishment blend in the absorbed

thought with a feeling that human affection never struggled more ardently, passionately, and triumphantly against the oblivion of Death. There is one sustained, harmonious, majestic sorrowfulness of pride in it, from the verse on the entrance which says that "the pure of heart shall enter the Gardens of God," to the small, delicate letters of sculptured Arabic upon the tomb-stone which tell, with a refined humility, that Mumtaz-i-Mahal, the "Exalted of the Palace," lies here, and that "Allah alone is powerful."

The Garden helps the Tomb, as the Tomb dignifies the Garden. It is such an orderly wilderness of rich vegetation as could only be had in Asia, broad flags of banana belting the dark tangle of banyan and bamboo, with the white pavements gleaming crosswise through the verdure. Yet if the Taj rose amid the sands of a dreary desert, the lovely edifice would beautify the waste, and turn it into a tender parable of the desolation of death, and the power of love, which is stronger than death. You pace round the four sides of the milk-white monument, pausing to observe the glorious prospect over the Indian plains, commanded from the platform on that face where Jumna washes the foot of the wall. Its magnitude now astounds. The plinth of the Taj is over one hundred yards each way, and it lifts its golden pinnacle two hundred and forty-four feet into the sky. From a distance this lovely and aerial dome sits therefore above the horizon like a rounded cloud. And having paced about it, and saturated the mind with its extreme and irresistible loveliness, you enter reverently the burial-place of the Princess Arjamund, to find the inner walls of the monument as much a marvel of subtle shadow and chastened light, decked with delicate jewellery, as the exterior was noble and simple. On the pure surface of this Hall of Death, and upon the columns, panels, and trellis-work of the marble screens surrounding the tomb, are patiently inlaid all sorts of graceful and elaborate embellishments — flowers, leaves, berries, scrolls, and sentences — in jasper, coral, bloodstone, lapis-lazuli, nacre, onyx, turquoise, sardonyx, and even precious gems. Moreover, the exquisite Abode of Death is haunted by spirits as delicate as their dwelling. They will not answer to rude noises, but if a woman's voice be gently raised in notes of hymn or song, if a chord is quietly sounded, echoes in the marble vault take up the music, repeat, diversify, and amplify it with strange combinations of melodious sounds, slowly dying away and re-arising, as if Israfil, "who has the sweetest voice of all Allah's angels," had set a guard of his best celestial minstrels to watch the death-couch of Arjamund. For, under the beautiful screens and the carved trellis-work of alabaster is the real resting-place of the "Exalted One of the Palace." She has the centre of the circular area, marked by a little slab of snow-white marble; while by her side — a span loftier in height, because he was man and Emperor, but not displacing her from the pre-eminence of her grace and beauty — is the stone which marks the resting-spot of Shah Jehan, her lord and lover. He has immortalised — if he could not preserve alive for one brief day — his peerless wife; yet the pathetic moral of it all is written in a verse hereabouts from the *Hudees,* or "traditions." It runs — after reciting the styles and titles of "His Majesty, King of Kings, Shadow of Allah, whose Court is as Heaven:" — *"Saith Jesus (on whom be peace), This world is a bridge! pass thou over it, but build not upon it! This world is one hour; give its minutes to thy prayers; for the rest is unseen."*

EDWIN ARNOLD
India Revisited, 1886

A LUSTROUS PEARL

A French novelist, a German philosopher, and a Swedish prince all fell under the spell of the Taj Mahal in the early years of the twentieth century. Pierre Loti, whose extensive travels around the world provided the backgrounds for his novels, made his pilgrimage to India in 1903.

Amongst the distant plains white cupolas, of that diaphanous pearliness that no artifice can ever imitate, are seen rising from the dusty haze that covers all the land, a haze which turns from blue to purple in the evening twilight. These are the resting-places of the princesses who once trod these lofty terraces, and, arrayed in gold-striped muslins and precious stones, displayed their naked loveliness. The largest dome is that of the Taj, Taj the incomparable, where the great sultana, Montaz-i-Mahal, sleeps since two hundred and seventy years ago. Everybody has seen and has described the Taj, which is known as one of the classic wonders of the world. Enamels and miniatures still preserve the features of the much beloved Montaz-i-Mahal and of her husband, the sultan, who created the place, wishing to enshroud his dead wife with unheard-of splendour. Standing in a park-like cemetery that is walled in like a fortress, the Taj is the largest and most stainless mass of marble that the world has seen. The walls of this park and the high cupolas rising over the four outer gates are of red sandstone encrusted with alabaster, but the artificial lakes, shady groves and boskages of palm and cypress that lie within display a cold formality of tracing. Out of these the incomparable monument towers forth in a whiteness which the surrounding sombre greenery seems to enhance. An immense cupola and four minarets, lofty as towers, stand on a white pediment, and everywhere the same restful purity of outline and the same calm and supremely simple harmony of tone, pervade a colossal edifice entirely built of white marble, diapered by almost imperceptible lines of a pale gray. . . .

Under the central cupola, which is seventy-five feet high, the sultana sleeps. Here there is nothing but the most superb simplicity, only a great white splendour. It should be dark here, but it is as light as if these whitenesses were self-illuminating, as if this great carved sky of marble had a vague transparence. There is nothing on the walls but veins of pearly gray and a few faintly outlined arches, and on the dome's white firmament nothing but those facets traced as with a compass, which imitate the crystal pendants of some stalactite cave. Around the pediment, however, there is a bordering of great lilies sculptured in bold relief. Their stalks seem to spring out of the ground, and the marble flowers look as if their petals were about to fall. This decoration, which flourished in India in the seventeenth century, has now been more or less indifferently imitated by our modern Western art.

The wonder of wonders is the white grille that stands in the centre of the translucent hall and incloses the tomb of the sultana. It is made of plaques of marble placed upright, so finely worked that it might be thought that they were carved in ivory. On each marble upright and each stud with which these fretted marble plaques are surrounded little garlands of tulips, fuchsias, and immortelles are worked in mosaics of turquoise, topaz, porphyry, or lapis lazuli. The sonority of this white mausoleum is almost terrifying, for the echoes never seem to cease.

PIERRE LOTI
India, 1903

Palace entrance in Delhi

Count Hermann Keyserling's three-year odyssey around the world included a stop in India. In The Travel Diary of a Philosopher, *written in 1914, the German mystic recorded his aesthetic and metaphysical thoughts on the Taj Mahal.*

I could not have believed that there could be anything like it. A massive marble structure without weight, as if composed of ether; perfectly rational and yet purely decorative; without ascertainable content, and yet full of significance in the highest degree: the Taj Mahal is not only one of the greatest works of art, it is perhaps the greatest of all pieces of artifice which the creative spirit of man has ever achieved. The maximum of perfection which seems to be attained here is beyond every gauge of which I know, for partly perfected achievements in the same direction do not exist. Structures of similar design are spread in dozens over the wide plain of Hindustan, but not one of them lets us even suspect the synthesis which is embodied in the foundation of Shah Dshehan. The others are rationally devised buildings, with beautiful decorations super-added; the reasonable element has its own effect, so has the decorative, and we can judge the whole from the same premises which apply to all architecture. The case of the Taj Mahal is unmistakably one of a change of dimension. Here the rational elements have been melted into the decorative, which means that gravity, whose exploitation is the real principle of all other architecture, has lost its weight; conversely, the decorative quality has been stripped of its arabesque-like nature, for here the arabesques have assimilated all reason and are possessed of the same mental significance which is usually the privilege of the rational. Thus, the Taj Mahal seems, not only beautiful, but simultaneously, strange as it may sound, marvellously pretty; it is the rarest of jewels. It lacks, in spite of perfect beauty, unrivalled loveliness and charm, all grandeur. And now as to its meaning: as far as the ordinary architectural possibilities of expression go, it lacks all expressive value, as much as any show specimen of the goldsmith's craft. It exhales neither intellectual sublimity, like the Parthenon, nor composure and strength, like the typical Mohammedan buildings. Its forms have neither a spiritual background, like those of Gothic cathedrals, nor an animalic, emotional one, like the Drawidian Temples. The Taj Mahal is not even necessarily a funeral monument: it might just as well, or just as badly, be a pleasure resort. . . .

Architecture is regarded as a fettered art; this is true in so far as spiritual beauty can only be represented in it through the medium of empirical appropriateness. That which seems to be beautiful without being appropriate is, for that reason, senseless and lacking in content — the arabesque is there and pleases us, but it means nothing. Hence the curious antagonism between the rational and decorative elements: in the case of a perfectly rational art, like that of the Greeks, the arabesque seems superfluous; the less decoration and accessories, the better. On the other hand, the decorative element necessarily needs an object which gives meaning to it. It strikes us as most substantial where it presupposes a life which corresponds with it, as in the palaces of Italy and India; the more independent significance it assumes, the emptier and more meaningless does it appear. In the case of the Taj Mahal the spirit does not seem fettered by matter, and the decorative elements do not seem empty of inner content; this building is absolutely purposeless, in spite of perfect rationality, and perfectly substantial in spite of its arabesque character. It belongs to a special sphere. . . .

And what is it which conditions its unique quality? It is the accumulated effect of many details; it is the existence of shades which we would never credit with the capacity for signifying so much. The general plan of the Taj Mahal is shared by hundreds of Indian mausoleums, whose effect is perfectly indifferent; its chromatics have been imitated a hundred times, with no better result than that the buildings thus decorated give the impression of a wedding cake. Let us transpose ever so slightly the proportions, or change its dimensions by an iota, or use a different material; or place the Taj Mahal, as it is, into another region which is subject to different conditions of air, damp and light: it would be the Taj Mahal no longer. I have seen the same white marble used for mosques not a hundred miles distant from Agra: it lacks the enamel-like quality of the Taj Mahal.

HERMANN KEYSERLING
The Travel Diary of a Philosopher, 1925

Main street of Agra

An explorer and the author of several travel books, Prince William, the son of King Gustavus V of Sweden, was enchanted by the mysterious Taj Mahal.

It was a warm moonlight evening, and in spite of the tiring journey we decided, as soon as we had had something to eat at the hotel and washed off the worst of the dust, to proceed at once to the far-famed Taj Mahal.

The whole city was already asleep, and the deserted roads wound like white ribbons through the dark foliage in the extensive gardens of the Cantonments, where the only creatures abroad were a few sleepy pack-camels, whose grotesque shadows jogged slowly along the dusty roadway. After about a quarter of an hour's drive we stopped, entered the broad gate in the wall that surrounds the sanctuary on all sides — and the Taj Mahal lay before us, gleaming white in the clear light of the moon.

How can my poor pen describe this masterpiece, which has already inspired so many poets and authors with lofty poems and ardent romances? . . .

Like a faultless, lustrous Oriental pearl the masterpiece among all the treasures of India lay dreaming, a white jewel enclosed in a frame of dark cypresses, with the flashing starry sky as a background. The soft lines of the mighty marble dome and the defiant elevation of the four minarets formed an organic whole, so perfect, so instinct with beauty, that one involuntarily passed a hand over one's eyes, wondering whether it was not merely a beautiful dream or an unreal image. Like glittering bands of silver the cool marble ponds extended up to the sanctuary, bordered on each side by lofty cypresses and climbing roses, with dark, luxuriant foliage behind. All was silent and still; not a rustle, not a whisper was heard, and the air was full of the scent of roses and lavender. Peace breathed from every stone, every flower, every quivering moonbeam; peace to the grave of the beloved, peace to the memory of Arjmand Banu! And the mind was irresistibly seized with a feeling of gratitude toward this woman, whose spirit seemed still to float beneath the lofty marble vaults, simply for having lived and been capable of inspiring a feeling deep and strong enough to be still perceptible to later generations after a lapse of centuries.

With lingering steps we approached the sanctuary — it seemed almost profane to tread these pavements with dusty shoes, where the Mohammedan believer never enters except barefooted — and passed devoutly through the

154

broad portal. From the roof of the mighty dome hung a flickering oil-lamp, and in the middle of the floor — surrounded by a most delicate grille of carved marble — stood the two splendidly carved and inlaid alabaster cenotaphs of Mumtaz Mahal (Arjmand Banu) and Shah Jehan. Wherever the eye turned in the great hall, it was met by the gleam of costly mosaics, and the interstices were carved with artistic reliefs. The echo was so powerful that a long-drawn "Allah-il-Allah" from one of the guardians was repeated a hundredfold in the lofty roof and still reverberated long after among the polished walls of the dome. A narrow flight of steps led down to the vault of the actual tomb, where the two coffins — also of alabaster — are placed exactly under the respective cenotaphs.

The stroke of midnight had long resounded before we could make up our minds to leave the enchanted spot. . . .

The next day . . . [was] devoted exclusively to sight-seeing at high pressure, and thanks to a good share of energy and constant running from one mosque to another, we managed to get through most of the sights, which as a rule take two days. But it was warm work, and I am sure we each left about two pounds of moisture on the pavements of the city.

We began with a short visit to the Taj, to get an impression of it by daylight. The sun shone so intensely on the dead-white marble that one was forced to look with half-closed eyes or to wear smoked glasses to avoid being dazzled. The many delicate details now appeared to greater advantage, and the inlaid work especially, with its wealth of stones of different colours, was seen to be masterly; but otherwise I preferred the lovely moonlight effect of the evening before with its atmosphere of profound feeling, and it is thus that I would choose to remember this costliest gem among all the treasures of India.

H.R.H. PRINCE WILLIAM OF SWEDEN
In the Lands of the Sun, 1915

DISSENTING VOICES

Rudyard Kipling's intimate knowledge of India — he was born in Bombay of English parents — served him well in his celebrated career as novelist, poet, and short-story writer. Adopting the guise of a globetrotter, the future Nobel laureate wrote travel pieces for the Civil & Military Gazette *and* Pioneer *in Lahore during the 1880's. Kipling's wry perspective captured not only the magnificence of the Taj Mahal, but also the posturing of the typical British tourist.*

Because he wished to study our winter birds of passage, one of the few thousand Englishmen in India on a date and in a place which have no concern with the story, sacrificed all his self-respect and became — at enormous personal inconvenience — a Globe-trotter going to Jeypore, and leaving behind him for a little while all that old and well-known life in which Commissioners and Deputy-Commissioners, Governors and Lieutenant-Governors, Aides-de-camp, Colonels and their wives, Majors, Captains, and Subalterns after their kind move and rule and govern and squabble and fight and sell each other's horses and tell wicked stories of their neighbours. But before he had fully settled into his part or accustomed himself to saying, "Please take out this luggage," to the coolies at the stations, he saw from the train the Taj wrapped in the mists of the morning.

There is a story of a Frenchman who feared not God, nor regarded man, sailing to Egypt for the express purpose of scoffing at the Pyramids and — though this is hard to believe — at the great Napoleon who had warred under their shadow. It is on record that that blasphemous Gaul came to the Great Pyramid and wept through mingled reverence and contrition; for he sprang from an emotional race. To understand his feelings it is necessary to have read a great deal too much about the Taj, its design and proportions, to have seen execrable pictures of it at the Simla Fine Arts Exhibition, to have had its praises sung by superior and travelled friends till the brain loathed the repetition of the word, and then, sulky with want of sleep, heavy-eyed, unwashed, and chilled, to come upon it suddenly. Under these circumstances everything, you will concede, is in favour of a cold, critical, and not too impartial verdict. As the Englishman leaned out of the carriage he saw first an opal-tinted cloud on the horizon, and, later, certain towers. The mists lay on the ground, so that the splendour seemed to be floating free of the earth; and the mists rose in the background, so that at no time could everything be seen clearly. Then as the train sped forward, and the mists shifted, and the sun shone upon the mists, the Taj took a hundred new shapes, each perfect and each beyond description. It was the Ivory Gate through which all good dreams come; it was the realisation of the gleaming halls of dawn that Tennyson sings of; it was veritably the "aspiration fixed," the "sign made stone" of a lesser poet; and over and above concrete comparisons, it seemed the embodiment of all things pure, all things holy, and all things unhappy. That was the mystery of the building. It may be that the mists wrought the witchery, and that the Taj seen in the dry sunlight is only, as guidebooks say, a noble structure. The Englishman could not tell, and has made a vow that he will never go nearer the spot, for fear of breaking the charm of the unearthly pavilions.

It may be, too, that each must view the Taj for himself with his own eyes, working out his own interpretation of the sight. It is certain that no man can in cold blood and colder ink set down his impressions if he has been in the least moved.

To the one who watched and wondered that November morning the thing seemed full of sorrow — the sorrow of the man who built it for the woman he loved, and the sorrow of the workmen who died in the building — used up like cattle. And in the face of this sorrow the Taj flushed in the sunlight and was beautiful, after the beauty of a woman who has done no wrong.

Here the train ran in under the walls of Agra Fort, and another train — of thought incoherent as that written above — came to an end. Let those who scoff at overmuch enthusiasm look at the Taj and thenceforward be dumb. It is well on the threshold of a journey to be taught reverence and awe.

But there is no reverence in the Globe-trotter: he is brazen. A Young Man from Manchester was travelling to Bombay in order — how the word hurts! — to be home by Christmas. He had come through America, New Zealand, and Australia, and finding that he had ten days to spend at Bombay, conceived the modest idea of "doing India." "I don't say that I've done it all; but you may say that I've seen a good deal." Then he explained that he had been "much pleased" at Agra, "much pleased" at Delhi, and, last profanation, "very much pleased" at the Taj. Indeed, he seemed to be going through life just then "much pleased" at everything.

RUDYARD KIPLING
From Sea to Sea, 1887

Audience hall in Delhi

Wonder and awe mark the reverent reactions of most visitors to the Taj Mahal. A notable and articulate dissenter was Aldous Huxley, the English novelist and satirist who is best known for his novels Brave New World *and* Point Counterpoint.

I am always a little uncomfortable when I find myself unable to admire something which all the rest of the world admires — or at least is reputed to admire. Am I, or is the world the fool? Is it the world's taste that is bad, or is mine? I am reluctant to condemn myself, and almost equally reluctant to believe that I alone am right. . . .

Here at Agra I find myself afflicted by the same sense of discomfort. The Taj Mahal is one of the seven wonders. My guide assures me that it is "perhaps the most beautiful building in the world." Following its advice, we drove out to have our first look at the marvel by the light of the setting sun. Nature did its best for the Taj. The west was duly red, and orange, and yellow, and, finally, emerald green, grading into pale and flawless blue towards the zenith. Two evening stars, Venus and Mercury, pursued the sunken sun. The sacred Jumna was like a sheet of silver between its banks. Beyond it the plains stretched greyly away into the vapours of distance. The gardens were rich with turf, with cypresses, palms, and peepul trees, with long shadows and rosy lights, with the noise of grasshoppers, the calling of enormous owls, the indefatigable hammering of a coppersmith bird. Nature, I repeat, did its best. But though it adorned, it could not improve the works of man. The Taj, even at sunset, even reverberated upside down from tanks and river, even in conjunction with melancholy cypresses — the Taj was a disappointment.

My failure to appreciate the Taj is due, I think, to the fact that, while I am very fond of architecture and the decorative arts, I am very little interested in the expensive or the picturesque, as such and by themselves. Now the great qualities of the Taj are precisely those of expensiveness and picturesqueness. Milk-white amongst its dark cypresses, flawlessly mirrored, it is positively the *Toteninsel* of Arnold Boecklin come true. And its costliness is fabulous. Its marbles are carved and filigreed, are patterned with an inlay of precious stones. The smallest rose or poppy on the royal tombs is an affair of twenty or thirty cornelians, onyxes, agates, chrysolites. The New Jerusalem was not more rich in variety of precious pebbles. If the Viceroy took it into his head to build another Taj identical with the first, he would have to spend as much as a fifteenth, or even perhaps a twelfth or tenth of what he spends each year on the Indian Army. Imagination staggers . . .

This inordinate costliness is what most people seem to like about the Taj. And if they are disappointed with it (I have met several who were, and always for the same reason) it is because the building is not quite so expensive as they thought it was. Clambering among the roofs they have found evidence to show that the marble is only a veneer over cheaper masonry, not solid. It is a swindle! Meanwhile the guides and guardians are earning their money by insisting on the Taj's costliness. "All marble," they say, "all precious stones." They want you to touch as well as look, to realise the richness not with eyes alone, but intimately with the fingers. I have seen guides in Europe doing the same. Expensiveness is everywhere admired. The average tourist is moved to greater raptures by St. Peter's than by his own St. Paul's. The interior of the Roman basilica is all of marble. St. Paul's is only Portland stone. The relative architectural merits of the two churches are not for a moment considered.

Architecturally, the worst features of the Taj are its minarets. These four thin tapering towers standing at the four corners of the platform on which the Taj is built are among the ugliest structures ever erected by human hands. True, the architect might offer a number of excuses for his minarets. He would begin by pointing out that, the dimensions of the main building and the platform being what they are, it was impossible to give the four subsidiary structures more than a certain limited mass between them, a mass small in proportion to the Taj itself. Architecturally, no doubt, it would have been best to put this definitely limited mass into four low buildings of comparatively large plan. But unfortunately, the exigencies of religion made it necessary to put the available mass into minarets. This mass being small, it was necessary that the minarets should be very thin for their height.

These excuses, so far as they go, are perfectly valid. By the laws of religion there had to be minarets, and by the laws of proportion the minarets had to be unconscionably slender. But there was no need to make them feebly taper, there was no need to pick out the component blocks of which they are built with edgings of black, and above all there was no need to surround the shaft of the minarets with thick clumsy balconies placed, moreover, at just the wrong intervals of distance from one another and from the ground.

The Taj itself is marred by none of the faults which characterize the minarets. But its elegance is at the best of a very dry and negative kind. Its "classicism" is the product not of intellectual restraint imposed on an exuberant fancy, but of an actual deficiency of fancy, a poverty of imagination. One is struck at once by the lack of variety in the architectural forms of which it is composed. There are, for all practical purposes, only two contrasting formal elements in the whole design — the onion dome, reproduced in two dimensions in the pointed arches of the recessed bays, and the flat wall surface with its sharply rectangular limits. When the Taj is compared with more or less contemporary European buildings in the neo-classic style of the High Renaissance and Baroque periods, this poverty in the formal elements composing it becomes very apparent. Consider, for example, St. Paul's. The number of component forms in its design is very large. We have the hemispherical dome, the great colonnaded cylinder of the drum, the flat side-walls relieved by square-faced pilasters and rounded niches; we have, at one end, the curved surfaces of the apse and, at the other, the West Front with its porch — a design of detached cylinders (the pillars), seen against a flat wall, and supporting yet another formal element, the triangular pediment. If it is argued that St. Paul's is a very much larger building than the Taj, and that we should therefore expect the number of contrasting elements in its design to be greater, we may take a smaller specimen of late Renaissance architecture as our standard of comparison. I suggest Palladio's Rotonda at Vicenza, a building somewhat smaller than the Taj and, like it, of regular design and domed. Analysing the Rotonda we shall find that it consists of a far larger number of formal elements than does the Taj, and that its elegance, in consequence, is much richer, much more subtle and various than the poor, dry, negative elegance characteristic of the Indian building.

But it is not necessary to go as far as Europe to find specimens of a more varied and imaginative elegance than that of the Taj. The Hindu architects produced buildings incomparably more rich and interesting as works of art. I have not visited Southern India where, it is said, the finest specimens of

Hindu architecture are to be found. But I have seen enough of the art in Rajputana to convince me of its enormous superiority to any work of the Mohammedans. The temples at Chitor, for example, are specimens of true classicism. They are the products of a prodigious, an almost excessive, fancy, held in check and directed by the most judicious intelligence. Their elegance — and in their way they are just as elegant as the Taj — is an opulent and subtle elegance, full of unexpected felicities. The formal elements of their design are numerous and pleasingly contrasted, and the detail — mouldings and ornamental sculpture — is always, however copious, subordinated to the architectural scheme and of the highest decorative quality.

In this last respect Hindu ornament is decidedly superior to that employed by the later Moguls. The *pietra dura* work at the Taj and the Shahdara tombs at Lahore is marvellously neat in execution and of extravagant costliness. These qualities are admirable in their way; but they have nothing to do with the decorative value of the work considered as art. As works of art, the *pietra dura* decorations of the Taj are poor and uninteresting. Arabesques of far finer design are to be seen in the carved and painted ornamentation of Rajput palaces and temples. As for the *bas reliefs* of flowers which adorn the gateway of the Taj — these are frankly bad. The design of them vacillates uncertainly between realism and conventionalism. They are neither life-like portraits of flowers nor good pieces of free floral decoration. How any one who has ever seen a fine specimen of decorative flower-painting or flower-carving, whether Hindu or European, can possibly admire these feebly laborious reliefs passes my understanding. Indeed, it seems to me that any one who professes an ardent admiration for the Taj must look at it without having any standards of excellence in his mind — as though the thing existed uniquely, in a vacuum. But the Taj exists in a world well sprinkled with masterpieces of architecture and decoration. Compare it with these, and the Imperial Mausoleum at once takes its proper place in the hierarchy of art — well down below the best. But it is made of marble. Marble, I perceive, covers a multitude of sins.

ALDOUS HUXLEY
Jesting Pilate, 1926

FIRST LADY'S PILGRIMAGE

Eleanor Roosevelt, one of America's most notable first ladies, served as a delegate to the United Nations from 1946 to 1952. Her abiding interest in international affairs then led her to embark upon a tour of the Middle East, India, Pakistan, and Nepal. In India, Mrs. Roosevelt marveled at the enduring perfection of the Taj.

I must own that by the time we got to Agra I was beginning to feel we had seen a great many forts and palaces and temples and mosques. I realized that I was no longer viewing them with the same freshness of interest and appreciation that I had felt during the early part of my visit. I think the others felt much the same way, which may have been one reason why we had all been talking more and more about the fact that no letters from home were reaching us. I had even cabled for news of my family. Therefore when we got back to Government House after our visit to Akbar's fort, though we knew we should leave immediately to get our first glimpse of the Taj Mahal at sunset, we all pounced on the letters we found waiting for us, and could not tear ourselves away until the last one had been read. Then, to our dismay, we found we had delayed too long; by the time we got to the Taj — about six-thirty — the light was beginning to fade.

What I have just said about feeling jaded cannot apply to the Taj. As we came through the entrance gallery into the walled garden and looked down the long series of oblong pools in which the Taj and the dark cypresses are reflected, I held my breath, unable to speak in the face of so much beauty. The white marble walls, inlaid with semiprecious stones, seemed to take on a mauve tinge with the coming night, and about halfway along I asked to be allowed to sit down on one of the stone benches and just look at it. The others walked on around, but I felt that this first time I wanted to drink in its beauty from a distance. One does not want to talk and one cannot glibly say this is a beautiful thing, but one's silence, I think, says this is a beauty that enters the soul. With its minarets rising at each corner, its dome and tapering spire, it creates a sense of airy, almost floating lightness; looking at it, I decided I had never known what perfect proportions were before. . . .

The white marble of the Taj symbolizes the purity of real love; and somehow love and beauty seem close together in this creation.

We returned in the evening to see it in the full moonlight, as everyone says you should, and though each time I saw it it was breath-taking, perhaps it was most beautiful by moonlight. We could hardly force ourselves to leave, and looked at it from every side, unable to make up our minds which was the most beautiful. I think though I liked my view from the bench halfway down the reflecting pools, possibly because water is so precious in India that it enhances everything.

Early the next morning — at seven-thirty to be exact — we visited the Taj again to see it in the clear daylight. It was still impressive and overwhelmingly lovely, but in a different way; and the marble looked slightly pinkish, as though it was being warmed by the sun.

As long as I live I shall carry in my mind the beauty of the Taj, and at last I know why my father felt it was the one unforgettable thing he had seen in India. He always said it was the one thing he wanted us to see together.

ELEANOR ROOSEVELT
India and the Awakening East, 1953

REFERENCE

Chronology of Indian History

1450	Lodi dynasty founded in Delhi
1498	Portuguese explorer Vasco da Gama rounds Cape of Good Hope and reaches Calicut on India's southwestern coast
1510	Portuguese acquire colony of Goa
1526	Baber defeats Ibrahim Lodi at battle of Panipat near Delhi and founds Mogul dynasty
1530	Humayun succeeds to throne upon Baber's death
1540	Afghan leader Sher Shah drives Humayun from India and founds Sur dynasty
1542	Birth of Akbar
1545	Death of Sher Shah
1555	With Persian aid, Humayun reoccupies Delhi and Agra and reestablishes Mogul rule over India
1556	Death of Humayun; accession of Akbar
1557–1601	Akbar consolidates Mogul power by conquest
1562	Akbar assumes personal rule
1564	Abolition of tax on Hindu pilgrims and repeal of the *jizya,* a poll tax on non-Moslems
1565	Construction of Red Fort at Agra
1569	Birth of Salim (later known as Jahangir)
1570	Foundations of city of Fatehpur Sikri laid
1573	Moguls conquer Gujarat
1575–82	Public debates on religion held
1576	Conquest of Bengal
1577	Fatehpur Sikri completed
1579	First Jesuit mission arrives in India
1582	Akbar decrees new religion of Din-i-Ilahi
1585	Fatehpur Sikri abandoned and entire court moved to Lahore
1586	Annexation of Kashmir
1600	East India Company granted charter for Indian trade by Queen Elizabeth I of England
1601–04	Jahangir rebels against Akbar but is restored to public favor
1602	United East India Company of the Netherlands formed for purposes of trade
1605	Upon death of Akbar, Jahangir crowns himself Mogul emperor
1609	Arrival of Englishman William Hawkins at Agra
1613	English win trading rights at Surat; marriage of Khurram (later, Shah Jahan) to Argumand Banu (later, Mumtaz Mahal)
1615	Arrival of Sir Thomas Roe, first English ambassador to Mogul court
1616–24	Bubonic plague ravages India
1618	Birth of Aurangzeb
1627	Death of Jahangir
1628	Peacock Throne built to commemorate coronation of Shah Jahan as Mogul emperor
1631	Death of Mumtaz Mahal
1632	Construction of Taj Mahal begun
1639	English acquire Madras
1643	Central Mausoleum of Taj Mahal completed
1647–59	Maratha leader Sivaji conquers parts of the Deccan
1654	Taj Mahal completed
1658	Aurangzeb seizes throne and imprisons Shah Jahan in the Red Fort at Agra
1658–81	Aurangzeb resides in Delhi
1661	Bombay acquired by the English
1664	French establish trading company in India
1666	Death of Shah Jahan
1670	Bombay replaces Surat as capital of British India
1674	French found Pondicherry
1678	Aurangzeb institutes severe political and religious repression of Hindus
1680	Death of Sivaji
1690	Calcutta founded by East India Company
1707	Death of Aurangzeb, last of the Great Moguls; empire begins to disintegrate as provincial rulers declare their independence
1707–12	Reign of Bahadur Shah
1712–19	Five puppet emperors reign successively
1715	East India Company gains right to trade in Bengal, to lease additional territory around Calcutta, and to coin money in Bombay
1719–48	Mohammed Shah rules empire from Delhi
1736	Persia conquered by Nadir Shah
1739	Nadir Shah invades Mogul Empire, sacks Delhi, massacres population, and departs for Persia with the Peacock Throne; weakened Mogul emperor rules in name only

1740	Deccan, Bengal, Bikar, Gujarat, Oudh, and Sind become independent
1746	French conquer Madras following outbreak of War of Austrian Succession in Europe
1748	Death of Mohammed Shah and accession of Ahmad Shah; by terms of Treaty of Aix-la-Chapelle, French return Madras to British
1756	Nadir Shah makes second expedition to Delhi; nawab of Bengal, Siraj-ud-daulah, captures English settlement of Calcutta and incarcerates prisoners in the "Black Hole of Calcutta"
1757	British forces led by Robert Clive retake Calcutta and defeat Siraj-ud-daulah at Plassey; victory makes British de facto rulers of Bengal
1759–1806	Reign of Shah Alam II
1760	Maratha army briefly occupies Delhi
1763	British supremacy over French in India secured by the Treaty of Paris
1764	Jats capture Agra, sack Red Fort, and carry off silver gates of the Taj Mahal; British victory at Buxor marks beginning of their military and political ascendancy in India
1765–67	Robert Clive administers Bengali affairs for East India Company
1773	Warren Hastings, first governor general of Bengal, introduces English law to India.
1787–1803	Governor General Richard Wellesley acquires most of the Deccan, Oudh, and Bengal
1803	Emperor Shah Alam II becomes pensioner of East India Company
1813	Parliament ends East India Company's monopoly of trade with India
1820	All of India except the Punjab under British rule
1828–33	Plan of Lord William Bentinck to demolish Mogul monuments, including the Taj Mahal, and auction their marble, is providentially canceled
1837–58	Reign of Bahadur Shah II
1848	British acquire Sikh territory
1849	British annex the Punjab
1857	Bengal army's native sepoys mutiny
1858	Sepoy Mutiny crushed; Britain assumes direct government of India; Bahadur Shah II, last of the Moguls, is deposed and exiled
1874	East India Company dissolved
1876	Red Fort at Delhi whitewashed for official visit of Prince of Wales
1877	Queen Victoria proclaimed empress of India
1885	Indian National Congress (later Congress Party) founded to promote Indian interests against the British
1899–1905	Lord Curzon sponsors restoration of the Taj Mahal
1920	Mohandas K. Gandhi (later known as the Mahatma), leader of the Indian National Congress, launches large-scale civil disobedience campaign to obtain self-government for India
1935	Government of India Act, passed by British Parliament, provides a form of limited self-government for India
1942–45	Indian National Congress, largely Hindu-supported, splits with Moslem League, which favors creation of a separate Moslem state of Pakistan
1947	Independence of India; Jawaharlal Nehru becomes first prime minister; Moslem regions secede and form Dominion of Pakistan; India acquires Moslem Kashmir following the end of a pro-Pakistan uprising
1948	Assassination of Gandhi by a Hindu fanatic
1949	India becomes a federal republic within the British Commonwealth
1952	First general elections in India held under universal suffrage
1961	Portuguese colony of Goa conquered by India
1962	China-Pakistan border war ends in cease-fire
1964	Death of Nehru
1965–66	Hostilities between India and Pakistan over Kashmir end with truce
1966	Mrs. Indira Gandhi elected leader of Congress Party and sworn in as prime minister
1971	East Pakistan declares its independence as the sovereign state of Bangladesh; India recognizes new government and provides military support; West Pakistani armed forces in Bangladesh surrender; influx of seven million refugees into India creates severe health and economic crisis
1972	Repatriation of nearly two million East Bengali refugees; Indian forces withdraw from Bangladesh

Guide to Mogul Monuments

The Mogul building arts, which reached their pinnacle with construction of the Taj Mahal, also spawned numerous other unique and fascinating works. Akbar and his immediate successors, Jahangir and Shah Jahan, drew upon the rich Persian artistic heritage of their Moslem religion and joined it with the singular skills of Indian craftsmen to forge a new architectural style. Although partisans on both sides still argue about the stylistic origins of particular buildings, the hybrid created by mixing these two traditions indisputably produced works of elegance and power.

The first major building of the Mogul era was **Humayun's Tomb**, located in Old Delhi. Traditionally the task of designing and supervising the construction of a mausoleum fell to the emperor himself. But construction on Humayun's tomb did not start until 1564, eight years after his death, and it is likely that Akbar's taste and artistic inclinations were responsible for the tomb's final shape.

In architectural quality the mausoleum represents one of the most harmonious blends of the Persian and Indian styles outside of the Taj itself. The building rests upon a 22-foot-high sandstone platform. At the center stands a room containing Humayun's burial crypt, flanked by chambers where his wife and other members of the royal family are buried. A slightly bulbous, Persian-style dome surmounts the structure; four kiosks, frequently employed as decorations by Indian architects, rim the dome. An innovation in the dome's construction was the use of a double shell—which allows the inner facing to be placed in proper proportion to the

room it covers while the outer shell rises to a graceful and imposing height. The entire structure is surrounded by a walled garden.

The energy and genius for which Akbar is remembered reveals itself more clearly in the massive building projects he commissioned: the forts at Agra, Lahore, and Allahabad, and the city of Fatehpur Sikri. These fortresses were more than mere military installations. Within their walls rose small cities occupied by the emperor and his entire

retinue—including his family, ministers of state, the women of the harem, and a complement of servants. Among the buildings usually found in these fortresses were reception halls, palaces, mosques, schools, and bathhouses—all were duplicated in each complex because there was no permanent central seat of government. As the emperor moved from Agra to Delhi to Lahore or to Kashmir, the government, lodged almost solely in his personage, moved with him.

The **Red Fort** at Agra stands on the

right bank of the Jumna River, surrounded by two massive red sandstone walls that stretch in a semicircle for a mile and a half. Although construction was begun in 1565 and officially completed by 1574, the complex underwent extensive changes during the reign of Shah Jahan, and thus many of its most important buildings are credited to him.

The palace called **Jahangir Mahal** is perhaps the most significant structure built by Akbar that has survived unaltered in the Red Fort. A large rambling building, it is thought to be a decidedly Hindu-style palace, especially because it lacks the carved arches seen in many other Mogul designs. Elaborate carvings on the façade and columns—and delicate green and blue tiling on the upper story—are a pleasant counterbalance to the palace's red sandstone bulk.

Akbar also directed the building of the Lahore and Allahabad forts. The **Lahore Fort,** built on an open plot of land, follows the shape of a parallelogram, with the interior space divided equally between royal living quarters and government offices. While the architectural style is very similar to that of the fort at Agra, the Lahore fortress is distinguished by remarkable tile decorations on the exterior of its northern wall. Pictures of sporting events—elephant fights, polo games, and hunting expeditions—as well as floral arrangements cover an area forty-eight yards long and seventeen yards high. Although the work is not dated, the method of construction suggests that it was added long after the structure was completed.

The complex built at Allahabad was the largest of the three forts built during

Akbar's regency. The **Allahabad Fort** is reputed to have been one of Akbar's favorite residences, but little is left of the structure, which was appropriated and largely destroyed by the British, who used it as an arsenal in the nineteenth century.

The city of **Fatehpur Sikri** is certainly the most unique part of Akbar's architectural legacy. Built on a site some twenty-three miles west of Agra, this pal-

ace complex was meant to pay homage to Shaikh Salim Chishti, who accurately predicted the birth of Akbar's heir, Jahangir. In the remarkably short span of four years, an entire capital city was constructed—and then, even more swiftly, it was abandoned. The court left Fatehpur Sikri in 1585, and the city was never again occupied. It stands today as a testament to the extravagant manner in which the Moguls wielded their power and wealth.

Of the many buildings at Fatehpur Sikri, a few are typical of the complex.

The **Diwan-i-Khas** was Akbar's private reception hall, the place where he interviewed diplomats, conferred with his ministers, and carried on discussions with religious leaders. This square building stands immediately opposite Akbar's private apartments, the Kwabagh. Outside, the Diwan-i-Khas appears to be a two-story building; upon entering the structure, one finds oneself in a single vaulted chamber. A gallery runs along the walls halfway between the floor and ceiling. At the center of the room stands a large carved column supporting a white marble platform, which is linked to the gallery by four railed passageways. Here Akbar sat upon his throne, his ministers and religious advisers attending him from the gallery and those seeking an audience standing on the floor below—a grand and dramatic throne room.

The building known as **Jodh Bai Palace** was one of the principle residences for women at Fatehpur Sikri. Enclosed within its plain, high wall were

facilities to accommodate every aspect of day-to-day life. The palace's single entrance was guarded by eunuchs, whose station was in turn protected by palace guards. Akbar gained entrance to the building by a private underground tunnel that led from his rooms to Jodh Bai Palace and other residences. As these precautions indicate, the women of the harem were carefully shielded from outside contacts.

The most grandiose structure at Fatehpur Sikri is the mosque known as **Jami Masjid**, the Great Mosque. The complex—a quadrangle that covers an area approximately 540 feet by 470 feet —consists of three separate parts: the tombs of Salim Chishti and Islam Khan, the south gateway known as the Buland Darwaza, and the mosque itself.

The mausoleums of Akbar's two most trusted religious advisers stand on the north side of the quadrangle. Both are built entirely of white marble, and the tomb of Salim Chishti in particular is covered with unusual stone carvings. The sacred sanctuary, with its three graceful domes and intricately carved pillars, stands at the west end of the courtyard.

The entire structure is dominated by the south gateway, the **Buland Darwaza**. Built in 1575 to commemorate Akbar's victorious Gujarat campaigns, it rises to truly majestic proportions, covering a space 130 feet long and 88 feet wide and soaring to a height of 134 feet. The architects managed to solve the problem of placing human-sized portals in such a large building by constructing a recessed semidome that balances the structure. Overall, the Buland Darwaza has a strongly Persian cast, with the exception, of course, of the kiosks that adorn the roof.

Akbar's Tomb, built at Sikandra, six miles northwest of Agra, is another product of his idiosyncratic taste. The mausoleum, which rests on a marble platform set in a 150-acre garden, has the appearance of a truncated pyramid —abruptly terminated after five stories,

each of which is covered with delicately wrought kiosks.

Jahangir did not emulate his father's taste for extravagant building schemes, although he was responsible for additions to the Lahore fort and he did supervise the construction of luxurious gardens at Lahore and Kashmir. The **Tomb of Itimad-ud-Dowlah,** Jahangir's prime minister and father-in-law, is considered an important transition between the bold architectural style of Akbar and the more delicate taste of Shah Jahan. The mausoleum, designed by Nur Mahal for her father, rests on the banks of the Jumna River in Agra. It is constructed entirely of white marble and is inlaid with semiprecious stones—introducing this technique to Mogul building. The shape of the tomb and the materials used in its construction mark Itimad-ud-Dowlah's tomb as having a strong Persian heritage.

All the Mogul rulers lavished great care on the design and construction of gardens—thereby creating perfect retreats that were soothing to the mind and spirit. Despite differences in detail, the gardens basically followed a highly stylized pattern. A rectangular space, enclosed within a substantial wall, was subdivided into four or more square parterres. Water ran down a canal that split the garden lengthwise and created gently cascading waterfalls. Pavilions were built over these falls to allow the emperor and his court to hear the restful flow of water and be cooled by its spray. In addition to central pavilions, the gardens included tree-shaded walkways, pergolas of vines and flowers, and open grassy areas for feasts and gatherings.

Shah Jahan's reign marked the true flowering of Mogul architectural abilities—culminating, of course, in the Taj Mahal. But other buildings, large and small, are equal testament to the superb taste of this ruler. At the Red Fort in Agra, for example, Shah Jahan rebuilt and expanded the **Diwan-i-Am,** the public audience hall, and the **Diwan-i-Khas,** the private audience hall, replacing much of the original sandstone used in the interiors of both buildings with white marble inlaid with colored stones.

Shielded behind a plain sandstone

wall in the Agra fort is one of the most exquisite mosques built by the Moguls. The **Pearl Mosque** was constructed entirely of white marble with two exceptions: yellow marble inlaid in the floor and an inscription in black over the entrance. Its interior is divided into three sections by a series of carved arches and pillars; three small bulbous domes and a row of kiosks crown the structure.

Outside Agra, Shah Jahan was responsible for the construction of the Red Fort at Delhi and one of the largest mosques built in India. The latter, also known as the **Jami Masjid,** is a less pleasing amalgam of the Indian and Persian styles than many of Shah Jahan's other buildings, but its large size and dominant position in the midst of the Delhi bazaar make it a significant work.

The Mogul leaders who followed Shah Jahan did not demonstrate a comparable taste and facility in the building arts, and the works they produced were of a decidedly inferior quality. But as the Taj Mahal alone so clearly demonstrates, the Mogul dynasty bequeathed to India a rich architectural heritage.

Selected Bibliography

Babur-nama in English. Translated by A. S. Beveridge. London: Luzac & Company, 1922.

Brown, Percy. *Indian Architecture.* Bombay: D. B. Taraporevala Sons & Company, 1942.

Cambridge History of India, vol. IV. Cambridge: Cambridge University Press, 1937.

Gascoigne, Bamber. *The Great Moghuls.* New York: Harper & Row, Publishers, 1971.

Hambly, Gavin. *Cities of Mughal India.* New York: G. P. Putnam's Sons, 1968.

Havell, E. B. *Indian Architecture.* London: John Murray Ltd., 1913.

Lane-Poole, Stanley. *Aurangzeb.* Oxford: Clarendon Press, 1893.

Moin ud-Din. *The Taj and Its Environments.* Agra: R. G. Bansal & Co., 1924.

Prasad, B. *History of Jahangir.* London: H. Milford & Co., 1922.

Prasad, Ishwari. *The Life and Times of Humayun.* Bombay: Orient Longmans, 1956.

Saksena, B. P. *A History of Shajahan of Dilhi.* Allahabad: Central Book Depot, 1962.

Spear, Percival. *Twilight of the Mughals.* Cambridge: Cambridge University Press, 1951.

Villiers, Stuart, C. M. *Gardens of the Great Mughuls.* London: A. and C. Black, 1913.

Welch, Stuart C. *The Art of Mughal India.* New York: The Asia Society Inc., 1963.

Acknowledgments and Picture Credits

The Editors make grateful acknowledgment for the use of excerpted material from the following works:

India and the Awakening East by Eleanor Roosevelt. Copyright 1953 by Anna Eleanor Roosevelt. The excerpt appearing on pages 159–60 is reproduced by permission of Harper & Row, Publishers, Inc.

Indian Journal by Edward Lear. Edited by Ray Murphy. Copyright 1955 by Ray Murphy. The excerpt appearing on page 149 is reproduced by permission of Jarrolds Publishers Ltd.

"Agra," from *Jesting Pilate* by Aldous Huxley. Copyright 1926 by Harper & Row, Publishers, Inc.; renewed 1953 by Aldous Huxley. The excerpt appearing on pages 157–59 is reproduced by permission of Harper & Row, Publishers, Inc.

The Editors would like to express their particular appreciation to Ellen Kavier of New York, who wrote the Guide to Mogul Monuments on pages 165–67. In addition, the Editors would like to thank the following organizations and individuals:

Penny Ash, London
India Office Library, London — Mildred Archer
Los Angeles County Museum of Art — Catherine Glynn
Barbara Nagelsmith, Paris
Lynn Seiffer, New York

The title or description of each picture appears after the page number (boldface), followed by its location. Photographic credits appear in parentheses. The following abbreviations are used:

(DC)	— (David Carroll)
IOL	— India Office Library, London
LACM	— Los Angeles County Museum of Art
MMA	— Metropolitan Museum of Art, New York
MFAB(DC)	— Museum of Fine Arts, Boston (David Carroll)
PW(DC)	— Prince of Wales Museum, Bombay (David Carroll)
RF (DC)	— Red Fort Museum, Delhi (David Carroll)
VA (JW)	— Victoria and Albert Museum, London (John Webb)

ENDPAPERS Detail of an embroidered satin coat from the court of Jahangir, early 17th century. VA(JW) HALFTITLE Symbol designed by Jay J. Smith Studio FRONTISPIECE The dome and minarets of the Taj Mahal. (DC) **9** Enameled and jeweled steel elephant goad, 19th century. VA(JW) **10** Two pilgrims entering the main archway of the Taj Mahal. (DC) **12–13** Painted cotton cushion cover, 17th century. MMA, Rogers Fund, 1928

CHAPTER I **14** Marble inlaid flowers from the tombs at the Taj Mahal. (DC) **16** Miniature of Akbar receiving Jahangir and Shah Jahan, from the period of Jahangir, 1605–27. MMA, Gift of Alexander Smith Cochran, 1913. **18** Detail of a miniature of Sher Afghan Khan. RF(DC) **19** top, Profile of Jahangir, from a presentation medal, 1611. British Museum; bottom, Miniature possibly showing Jahangir embracing Nur Mahal, ca. 1615. LACM, Nasli and Alice Heeramaneck Collection **20** Sketch of Prince Shahriyar, 1605–27. RF(DC) **21** Miniature of Jahangir and his five sons, early 17th century. PW(DC) **22** Miniature of Jahangir weighing Prince Khurram against gold, ca. 1615. British Museum **23** left, Jeweled rock-crystal lime box, mid-17th century. LACM, Nasli and Alice Heeramaneck Collection; right, Gold and jeweled jade turban ornament, 17th century. VA(JW) **25** Miniature of the death of Khan Jahan Lodi, from a *Shah Jahan Namah* by Abid. Windsor Castle Library **26–27** The Taj Mahal from the top of the main gateway. (DC)

CHAPTER II **28** Marble inlaid flowers from the tombs at the Taj Mahal. (DC) **30** Detail of a miniature of a battle, from a *Baber Namah*. National Museum, Delhi (DC) **31** Map by Francis & Shaw, Inc. **32** Detail of a sketch for a miniature of Emperor Baber and a courtier in camp. RF(DC) **33** Detail of a miniature of Emperor Humayun. RF(DC) **34** Miniature of the young Akbar wrestling before the emperor. Bodleian Library, Oxford, Ms. Ousley, Add. 171 fol 13v **35** Miniature of Adham Khan being thrown from a palace balcony, from an *Akbar Namah* by Miskina and Sankar. VA (JW) **36** left, Sketch for a miniature of Akbar. MFAB(DC); center and right, Obverse and reverse of a coin minted during period of Akbar. British Museum **38** Miniature of Abu-l Fazl presenting his books to Akbar, ca. 1605 from an *Akbar Namah* by Nar Singh. Chester Beatty Library, Dublin, Ms. 3 fol 176v **39** Miniature of the Jesuits, Aquaviva, and Henriquez debating in the Ibadat Khana, ca. 1605, from an *Akbar Namah* by Nar Singh. Chester Beatty Library, Dublin, Ms. 3 fol 263v **40** Detail of a sketch for a miniature of Shaikh Salim Chishti. RF(DC) **42** Lotus Throne in Fatehpur Sikri. (DC) **43** Entrance gate at Fatehpur Sikri. (DC) **44–45** Miniature of Akbar visiting musicians in the woods. PW(DC) **46** Miniature of Jahangir and ShahAbbas by Abu-l Hasan, ca. 1620. Freer Gallery of Art, Smithsonian Institution **47** Drawing of a tower of heads from Peter Mundy's *Journal,* 1632. Bodleian Library, Oxford, Ms. Rawl. A 315 fol 40v. **48** Miniature of Jahangir handing a book to Shaikh Husain in presence of King James I, by Bichitr, ca. 1625. Freer Gallery of Art, Smithsonian Institution **50–51** Detail of a miniature of Akbar and Jahangir at a tiger hunt, 17th century. RF(DC) **52–53** Tomb of Itimad-ud-Dowlah, Agra. (DC) **54** Miniature of squirrels in a tree, by Abu-l Hasan, ca. 1615. IOL, J. 1.30 **55** left, Watercolor of a zebra, attributed to Mansur, ca. 1620. VA(JW); right, Miniature of Jahangir, by Bichitr. Chester Beatty Library, Dublin.

CHAPTER III **56–57** Marble inlaid flowers from the tombs at the Taj Mahal. (DC) **58–59** top, Water buffalo at the Jumna River. (DC); bottom, Watermelon fields along the bank of the Jumna River. (DC); right, Flat-bottomed boat on the Jumna River. (DC) **60** Inscription from the Koran on the interior walls of the Taj Mahal. (DC) **63** Miniature of a crew building a Mogul structure, ca. 1580. VA(JW) **64** Terrace surrounding the Taj Mahal. (DC) **65** Pilgrims removing shoes before entering the Taj Mahal. (DC)

CHAPTER IV **66–67** Marble inlaid flowers from the tombs at the Taj Mahal. (DC) **68** Jeweled jade dagger, mid-17th century. LACM, Nasli and Alice Heeramaneck Collection **69** Miniature of Shah Jahan on the Peacock Throne, by Nadir al-Zaman, 17th century. MMA, Gift of Alexander Smith Cochran, 1913 **70** Miniature of a Sufi, ca. 1600. MFAB(DC) **71** Sketch for a miniature of Prince Khurram. RF(DC) **72** top, Enamel cameo of Shah Jahan killing a lion, mid-17th century. Bibliothèque Nationale, Paris, No. 366; bottom, Miniature of Shah Jahan on the Peacock Throne. British Museum, Ms. Add. 20.734 ff. fols 689–90 **73** Miniature of a poet or Sufi in a garden, ca. 1610. MFAB(DC), Goloubew Collection **74** Detail of a miniature of Shah Jahan and his three sons watching an elephant fight. RF(DC) **75** Miniature of Jahangir watching an elephant fight, 1605–27. MMA, Rogers Fund, 1912 **76–77** Detail of a miniature of a prince with his advisers and concubines, 17th century. PW(DC) **78** Miniature of a young girl, mid-17th century. IOL, Johnson Album XIII, fol 6 **79** Miniature of a eunuch, 17th century. MFAB(DC) **80** Detail of a miniature of the wedding of Shah Jahan's son, 1620–30. National Museum, Delhi (DC) **83** Spread showing party of Europeans at an Indian court, ca. 1650. VA (JW) **84** Drawing of Shah Jahan using a matchlock, mid-17th century. Chester Beatty Library, Dublin Ms. III, (b)IV **86** Miniature of Shah Jahan, mid-17th century. PW(DC) **87** The Taj Mahal as seen from the Jasmine Pavilion at the Red Fort. (DC)

CHAPTER V **88** Marble inlaid flowers from the tombs at the Taj Mahal. (DC) **90** Frontal view of the Taj Mahal. (DC) **91** Plan by Francis & Shaw, Inc. **92–93** left, The main gateway to the Taj Mahal. (DC); right, The top of the main gateway to the Taj Mahal. (DC) **94** The dome of the Taj Mahal. (DC) **95** Indian haystack. (DC) **96** The ja-wab at the Taj Mahal. (DC) **97** The gardens at the Taj Mahal. (DC) **98** The tombs of Mumtaz Mahal and Shah Jahan at the Taj Mahal. (DC) **99** A minaret at the Taj Mahal. (DC) **100** A sweeper at the Taj Mahal. (DC) **101** The tomb of Mumtaz Mahal at the Taj Mahal. (DC)

CHAPTER VI **102** Marble inlaid flowers from the tombs at the Taj Mahal. (DC) **104** Jeweled jade sword handle, 18th century. VA(JW) **104–105** left, Ivory chessmen depicting Rajput warriors, etc., ca. 1800. VA(JW); right, Lacquered box from the Deccan, ca. 1670. VA(JW) **107** Maratha sword and sheath, 19th century. VA(JW) **108** Detail of a miniature of Aurangzeb slaying an elephant, 19th century. RF(DC) **109** Detail of a miniature of the aged Aurangzeb carried on a palanquin to the battle of Golconda, 1685. RF(DC) **110** left, Miniature of Bahadur Shah. IOL, Ms. Add. Or. 3108; right, Watercolor portrait of Jahandar Shah. IOL Ms. Add. Or. 2683 **111** left, Miniature of Farrukhsiyar. VA; right, Miniature of Mohammed Shah. IOL Ms. Add. 3110 **112–13** Painting of Hindu pilgrims visiting a Sivaite temple, ca. 1760. IOL, Add. Or. 483. **114** Painting of Mohammed Shah in a palanquin, ca. 1730. MFAB, Arthur Mason Knapp Fund. **115** Detail of a miniature showing opium eaters. RF(DC) **117** Miniature of Nadir Shah, 1736–47. VA(JW)

CHAPTER VII **118** Marble inlaid flowers from the tombs at the Taj Mahal. (DC) **120** Carved wooden effigy of Sultan Tipoo's tiger mauling a British East India Company employee. VA **121** Painting of Ashraf Ali Khan smoking a hookah, ca. 1760–63. IOL, Add. Or. 736 **122** Engraving of Lord Clive. IOL **123** Bust of Warren Hastings, by Thomas Banks, 1790. IOL **124–25** above, Watercolor showing the Old Fort, the Playhouse, and the Black Hole Monument, by Thomas Daniell from *Views of Calcutta, 1786–88.* IOL; below, Watercolor of the Old Court House and the Writers' Building by Thomas Daniell from *Views of Calcutta, 1786–88.* IOL **126–27** Two engravings of the Sepoy Mutiny, from Atkinson's *Campaign in India.* IOL **128–29** Painting of Sir David Ochterlony at home in India, ca. 1820. IOL Add. Or. 2 **130** Bust of Queen Victoria, by J. E. Bolhm, ca. 1887. National Portrait Gallery, London **132** Painting of the Taj Mahal on ivory, 19th century. PW(DC) **132–33** Watercolor of troops leaving the Red Fort, ca. 1830. IOL Add. Or. 332. **135** Engraving of the Taj Mahal overgrown with weeds, 19th century. (DC)

THE TAJ MAHAL IN LITERATURE **136** Illuminated page from a book that belonged to Shah Jahan. MMA, Kevorkian Foundation and Rogers Fund, 1955 **138–57** Engravings from R. Montgomery Martin's *The Indian Empire,* London 1858–61.

REFERENCE **165–67** Government of India Tourist Office.

Index